THE CARNIVORE
— DIET —
Made Easy!

**ACHIEVE OPTIMAL HEALTH AND BOOST WEIGHT LOSS
WITH SCIENCE-BACKED STRATEGIES, SIMPLE MEAL PLANS
AND MOUTHWATERING, MEAT-BASED RECIPES**

©Copyright 2024 - BH Publishing Group LLC

All rights reserved. The content within this book may not be reproduced, duplicated or transmitted without direct written permission from the author or the publisher. Under no circumstances will any blame or legal responsibility be held against the publisher, or author, for any damages, reparation, or monetary loss due to the information contained within this book, either directly or indirectly. You are responsible for your own choices, actions, and results.

Legal Notice:

This book is copyright protected. This book is only for personal use. You cannot amend, distribute, sell, use, quote or paraphrase any part of the content within this book, without the consent of the author or publisher.

Disclaimer Notice:

Please note the information contained within this document is for educational and entertainment purposes only. All effort has been expended to present accurate, up-to-date, and reliable, complete information. No warranties of any kind are declared or implied. Readers acknowledge that the author is not engaging in the rendering of legal, financial, medical or professional advice. The content within this book has been derived from various sources. Please consult a licensed professional before attempting any techniques outlined in this book. By reading this document, the reader agrees that under no circumstances is the author responsible for any losses, direct or indirect, which are incurred as a result of the use of the information contained within this document, including but not limited to, errors, ommisions or inaccuracies.

CONTENTS

ME 3
INTRODUCTION 9

CHAPTER

1 HOW DID WE GET OFF TRACK? 13
2 THE NUTRITIONAL POWER OF MEAT 23
3 THE ROOT PROBLEMS WITH PLANTS 33
4 ANSWERING COMMON QUESTIONS 43
5 LET FOOD HEAL YOU: A FRESH PERSPECTIVE 55
6 LET'S BEGIN: TAKING THE FIRST STEPS 67
7 REAL LIFE TESTIMONIES 93
8 WHY VEGANISM FALLS SHORT 103
9 BUDGET FRIENDLY CARNIVORE 113
10 30 DAYS OF CARNIVORE MEALS 119
11 MOUTHWATERING CARNIVORE RECIPES 132
12 RESOURCES 185

MOUTHWATERING RECIPES

BREAKFAST

The Best Omelette	134
Breakfast Casserole	135
Crepes	136
Breakfast Bowl	137
Biscuits	138
Breakfast Bombs	139
Scotch Eggs	140
Bacon and Brie Frittata	141
Bacon-Wrapped Egg Bites	142
Egg and Bacon Muffins	143
Bacon and Gruyère Sous Vide Egg Bites	144

LUNCH

Quiche	146
Salmon Patties	147
Bacon, Burger & Eggs	148
Chaffles	149
Fried Chicken Strips	151
Loaded Chicken Salad	152
Egg Salad	153
Ground Turkey Muffins	154
Egg Roll with Salmon and Cheese sauce	155
Deviled Eggs	156
Creamy Chicken Soup	157
Pork Rind Tortillas	158

DINNER

Juicy Baked Chicken Thighs	160
Parmesan Crusted Salmon	161
Pizza	162
Parmesan Meatballs	163
Meatloaf	164
Hearty Chili	165
Crispy Baked Chicken Wings	166
Bacon Cheeseburger Pie	167
Bacon Wrapped Sea Scallops	168
Creamy Alfredo Sauce	169

SNACKS & EXTRAS

Fried Mozzarella Sticks	172
Creamy Popsicles	173
Ice Cream	174
Cream Cheese Bites	175
Creamy Dreamy Custard	176
Carnivore White Bread	177
Creamy Mayonnaise	179
Bone Marrow	180
Bacon-Wrapped Liver Bites	181
Cinnamon Crunch Treat	182
Nutricious Bone Broth	183

ME

I first became aware of the importance of eating good food when my best friend said she had cancer. At 26, she looked to be in good health! How could this be happening? She then proceeded to tell me that "all the food we are eating is poison." I found that hard to believe. Poison? Why am I even alive? Still, that phrase struck a chord and I watched her treat this aggressive cancer with food and supplements. She eventually won the battle and I began to look at food differently.

I've always been somewhat slender but secretly battled with food. I would overeat when no one was looking. In college, after breaking up with a boyfriend, I began to have a very unhealthy relationship with food. I would make a batch of my favorite cookies and eat the whole bowl of cookie dough in one sitting. I would be fine during the day but when night came, the uncomfortable feelings of sadness began and I turned to food for comfort. Eventually I stopped buying key ingredients for my cookies but that didn't stop me from making weird versions and overeating that batch too. After quickly gaining 30 pounds in two months, I joined Weight Watchers and was able to lose most of the weight. But I still harbored an unhealthy attitude towards food. I remember sneaking into the kitchen at my in-laws in the middle of the night and eating half of a bag of M&Ms because I was too embarrassed to eat the amount that I really wanted in front of my new husband.

Looking back, I can see how it started. I was raised in a home where my mother was always unhappy with her size. She would diet by skipping meals and then ravenously eat half of a cake when no one was looking. Obviously, I had picked up her habits and struggled to not be obsessed with food. Over the years I maintained my weight by jumping from diet to diet, never really conquering my addictions to sugar and carbs. Sometimes I would go to sleep and think "Yay, I get to get up and eat!" Salty snacks never satisfied me, and I could eat sweets until I was sick

OVER THE YEARS I MAINTAINED MY WEIGHT BY JUMPING FROM DIET TO DIET, NEVER REALLY CONQUERING MY ADDICTIONS TO SUGAR AND CARBS.

and still wish for more. As I got older, it became more and more difficult to shed the extra pounds and resist the unhealthy food. I watched my calories, counted steps, and increased my cardio, but nothing worked. My tummy was morning, was unable to squat down without hurting and all of his joints ached. This was a shock as he has always been very active and healthy. Thankfully, his doctor suggested an elimination diet, which, unbeknownst to us, is

I WATCHED MY CALORIES, COUNTED STEPS, AND INCREASED MY CARDIO BUT NOTHING WORKED.

poochy, my jeans were too tight, and I was always hungry. Keto was an improvement, and I could lower my weight a small amount, but the counting and measuring was exhausting, and I still had an insatiable salty and sweet tooth. I was longing for a simpler, healthier, more effective way to eat.

Meanwhile, my husband, who is a reasonably fit guy, started complaining about being in pain all the time. He felt terrible every

basically Carnivore.
After cutting out all carbs and dairy (some people are allergic to dairy even though it is included in the carnivore diet) he noticed an improvement. After a month, his pain was gone, he had dropped 10 pounds, and as a bonus, his stomach was noticeably flatter. At first, we were eating two different meals, but eventually, I went ahead and ate what he ate just to keep life simple. After several weeks I noticed that I felt terrific, had dropped a little weight and my

KETO WAS AN IMPROVEMENT AND I COULD LOWER MY WEIGHT A SMALL AMOUNT BUT THE COUNTING AND MEASURING WAS EXHAUSTING

poochy tummy was gone as well! Even better, my cravings for sugar dropped dramatically and I felt satisfied all day long. No more afternoon slumps or shakes from the drop in blood sugar and it suddenly occured to me that I wasn't always thinking about food! I ate when I was hungry, stopped when I was full and felt a steady amount of energy throughout the day. My relationship with food was finally appropriate, and it felt so good! Since then, I pretty much eat carnivore 24/7 with an occasional treat of a glass of wine or sweet potato fries but I don't feel deprived or like I am missing out! Nothing is better than a juicy steak or a medium rare burger (no bun, of course!). The food is SO delicious and I can eat as much as I want to! Also, when Chris went back to the doctor after a few months on the diet, the numbers from his blood work had improved across the board. At ages 66 and 69, neither one of us takes any medications, which is not the norm for people our age. It's hard to believe that about 70% of adults in the U.S. are taking at least one prescription med every day, and nearly a quarter of people are on four or more! This is because they are suffering from chronic issues like diabetes, heart disease, and high blood pressure, especially for those getting up there in age. In addition, over 42% of adults are considered obese – that's more than 100 million people dealing with

I SUDDENLY NOTICED THAT I WASN'T THINKING ABOUT FOOD AT ALL!

NOTE

MORE THAN 2 IN 5 ADULTS
(ABOUT 42%)
are considered obese, according to the CDC.

weight issues! Crazy, right? These are alarming statistics, to be sure! I can't help but wonder if a change from the Standard American Diet to a diet of meat would restore our health and quality of life! I hope that, as you read through this book, you will catch a vision for your own health and wellness, and consider finding your best self through the carnivore path! Let's do this together!

AS OF 2023 APPROXIMATELY 70 PERCENT OF U.S. ADULTS TAKE AT LEAST 1 PRESCRIPTION DRUG DAILY WITH AROUND 24 PERCENT TAKING 4 OR MORE PRESCRIPTION MEDICATIONS.

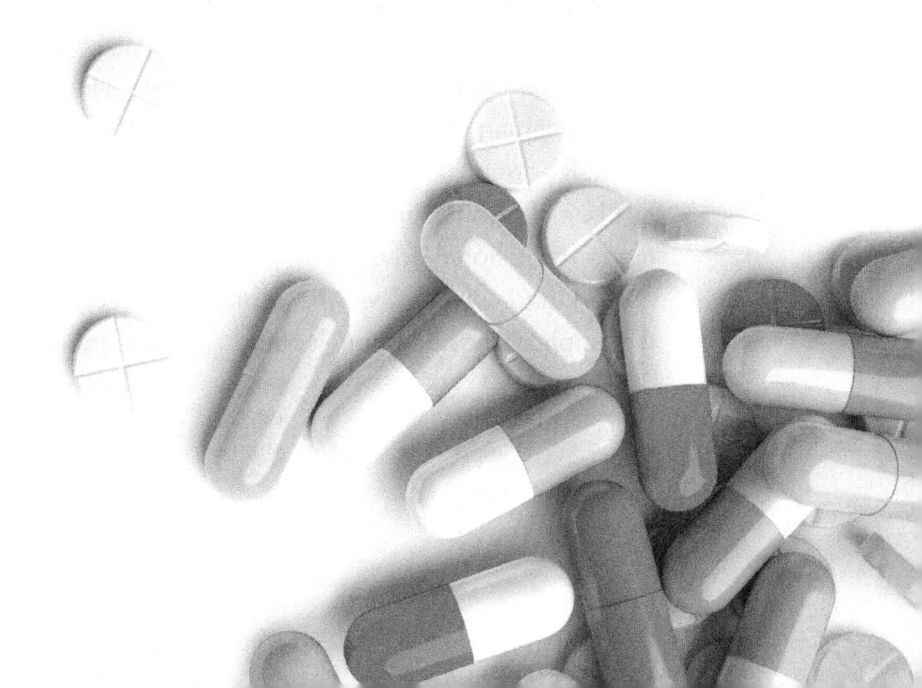

INTRODUCTION

REDISCOVERING HEALTH

The idea of eating an all-meat diet may seem radical, even outrageous, especially in a world that continually pushes the notion of balanced, plant-based eating, with a rainbow of fruits and vegetables. Yet, here we are, rediscovering a way of eating that is as old as humanity itself—one that's built on simplicity, nutrient density, and a complete focus on animal-based foods. Welcome to the world of the carnivore diet.

the rainbow," filling our plates with vegetables, grains, and plant-based products. But what if the very foods we've been told are the foundation of good health are contributing to chronic diseases, inflammation, and obesity? What if, instead of adding more complexity to our plates, the answer lies in simplicity?

The carnivore diet isn't just about meat. It's about healing. It's about

THE CARNIVORE DIET ISN'T JUST ABOUT MEAT. IT'S ABOUT HEALING. IT'S ABOUT REMOVING THE FOODS THAT IRRITATE OUR BODIES, TRIGGER AUTOIMMUNE RESPONSES, AND DISRUPT OUR GUT HEALTH.

This book is not about following a fad or jumping on the latest wellness trend. It's about exploring a diet that has been forgotten in the shuffle of modern nutritional advice and processed food culture. Over the years, the emphasis has been on "eating

removing the foods that irritate our bodies, trigger autoimmune responses, and disrupt our gut health. By eliminating plant-based foods, processed carbohydrates, and sugars, people across the globe have found relief from chronic health ailments that modern medicine and conventional diets have failed to address. Conditions like autoimmune disorders, digestive problems, obesity, mental health foods like beef, eggs, and organ meats, to breaking down the science of why plant toxins and carbohydrates can wreak havoc on our health, we'll explore why this

YOU'LL LEARN HOW THE BIOAVAILABILITY OF NUTRIENTS IN ANIMAL FOODS FAR SURPASSES THOSE IN PLANT-BASED SOURCES

disorders, and even chronic fatigue have been dramatically improved by adopting an animal-based approach to nutrition.

This book will explain the foundations of the carnivore diet, and how and why it works for so many people. From understanding the role of nutrient-dense animal

approach to eating is helping thousands reclaim their vitality.

Throughout this journey, you'll also hear from real people who have transformed their lives through the carnivore diet. Their stories of overcoming lifelong health struggles, like weight gain, autoimmune disorders, and even mental health issues, will inspire and show you that this way of eating isn't just a theory—it's a lifestyle with real, life-changing benefits.

As we dig deeper, we'll debunk common myths about cholesterol, heart disease, and vitamin deficiencies that have plagued modern nutritional discourse for decades. You'll learn how the bioavailability of nutrients in animal foods far surpasses those in plant-based sources and why the body can thrive when fueled by meat, fat, and organs.

Transitioning to the carnivore diet may feel daunting, especially when it goes against everything we've been taught about "balanced" nutrition. But by the end of this book, you'll have the tools, science, and confidence to make the leap, whether for a trial period or a complete lifestyle overhaul. We'll guide you through how to get started, what to expect during the transition, and how to customize the diet to fit your needs and goals.

The carnivore diet isn't for everyone, but for those who embrace it, the results can be transformative. Whether you're here out of curiosity, a desire to improve your health, or sheer frustration with diets that haven't worked for you, this book will serve as your guide to the carnivore lifestyle. You'll find everything you need to know to make informed decisions backed by science, personal stories, and real-life success.

So, let's strip away the confusion and complexity that's surrounded modern nutrition for far too long. Let's get back to basics. It's time to reclaim your health, rebuild your body, and rediscover the power of simplicity through the carnivore diet.

Welcome to the journey of healing, transformation, and empowerment—one steak at a time.

WELCOME TO THE JOURNEY OF HEALING, TRANSFORMATION, AND EMPOWERMENT, ONE STEAK AT A TIME.

CHAPTER 1

HOW DID WE GET OFF TRACK?

For decades, we've been overwhelmed with nutritional advice, yet the rates of chronic illnesses like obesity, diabetes, and heart disease continue to rise. Something in our approach to diet has gone terribly wrong. Our understanding of what constitutes a healthy diet has led us astray, and the consequences are evident in the declining health of so many. In this chapter, we'll explore how conventional dietary guidelines may have missed the mark and why much of what we've been taught about nutrition is outdated or misleading. Let's break down the key issues and examine a fresh perspective on where we've gone wrong.

IS NUTRITION REALLY THAT COMPLICATED?

Nutrition today feels like a complex puzzle. We're told to eat some of everything—fruits, vegetables, grains, lean meats, and healthy fats. We count calories, track macros, and obsess over every bite. Entire industries exist to help us manage our food intake with apps, books, and diets designed to guide us through this "complicated" maze. But is it really that difficult?

The reality is that nutrition was never supposed to be this hard. Our ancestors didn't have apps to measure their caloric intake. They didn't debate whether carbs were evil or whether fat would clog their arteries. Instead, they ate what was available, which was often animal-based foods. These simple, nutrient-dense foods fueled them for generations without the health problems we face today.

So, how did we get from a basic, meat-heavy diet that worked for our ancestors to the modern, carb-loaded, highly processed food landscape we live in today? A big part of the problem is that nutrition has been complicated by conflicting advice, much of it shaped by industries and governments with their own interests in mind.

It's often suggested that modern diets have drifted away from focusing on what truly matters for health: nutrient density and simplicity. Instead of constantly pursuing the latest diet fads or meticulously tracking macronutrient ratios, returning to the basic principles that have sustained humans for millennia may be more beneficial. By focusing on whole, nutrient-dense foods, we can simplify our approach to eating and prioritize what our bodies naturally thrive on.

BAD FAT

CHALLENGING THE FEAR OF FAT

For decades, we've been taught that fat—especially saturated fat—is the villain behind heart disease, weight gain, and clogged arteries. The famous "diet-heart hypothesis" from the mid-20th century, which suggested that eating foods high in saturated fat leads to high cholesterol and, subsequently, heart disease, has dominated dietary guidelines for years. This fear of fat led to the rise of low-fat diets, the promotion of seed and vegetable oils, and a massive increase in carbohydrate consumption. But what if that theory is wrong?

Recent research is poking holes in this assumption. Studies now show that the relationship between dietary fat and heart disease is much more complex than previously thought. Large-scale reviews have found little evidence to support the idea that saturated fat increases the risk of heart disease. On the contrary, some forms of cholesterol are protective. So, where does that leave us?

The problem with the diet-heart hypothesis is that it relied on cherry-picked data. Early researchers ignored evidence that didn't fit their narrative, leading to flawed conclusions that have shaped public policy for decades.

THIS FEAR OF FAT LED TO THE RISE OF LOW-FAT DIETS, THE PROMOTION OF SEED & VEGETABLE OILS, AND A HUGE INCREASE IN CARBOHYDRATE CONSUMPTION.

VS

Humans have been consuming animal fats—rich in saturated fats—for millennia, long before the rise of modern diseases.

Now, researchers are finding that cholesterol, especially LDL (often called the "bad" cholesterol), isn't the enemy. Instead, inflammation is the root cause of many chronic diseases, including heart disease. And guess what? High-carb, processed foods are often the culprits behind that inflammation. A meat-based diet, rich in animal fats, can reduce inflammation and improve health markers like cholesterol and blood pressure. It might be time to rethink what we've been taught about fat and cholesterol. These outdated beliefs have led to an epidemic of poor health.

INFLAMMATION IS THE ROOT CAUSE OF MANY CHRONIC DISEASES INCLUDING HEART DISEASE

DO WE REALLY NEED TO EAT OUR VEGETABLES?

"Eat your vegetables" has been a mantra for decades. We've been taught that vegetables are loaded with fiber, antioxidants, and essential vitamins that our bodies need. But what if they're not the miracle foods we've been led to believe? While eliminating vegetables may not be necessary for everyone, there's growing skepticism about whether they are truly essential for good health.

Many people feel better when they eliminate vegetables from their diets, particularly those with autoimmune conditions, gut issues, or chronic inflammation. That's because many vegetables contain substances called "anti-nutrients," like oxalates, phytates, and lectins. These compounds can interfere with nutrient absorption and cause problems for people with sensitive systems. For instance, oxalates, found in spinach and almonds, can contribute to kidney stones and joint pain in susceptible individuals. Phytates in whole grains and legumes can block the absorption of minerals like calcium, magnesium, and iron. While these anti-nutrients might not affect everyone, they're worth considering if you're dealing with health issues that don't seem to improve despite eating a "healthy" plant-based diet.

Additionally, while vegetables

NOTE

PLANT ANTI-NUTRIENTS

OXALATES
PHYTATES
LECTINS

Can block the absorption of nutrients in some plants

PHYTATES, PRESENT IN WHOLE GRAINS AND LEGUMES, CAN BLOCK THE ABSORPTION OF MINERALS LIKE CALCIUM, MAGNESIUM, AND IRON.

do contain some vitamins and minerals, they are often not as bioavailable as the nutrients found in animal products. For example, the iron in spinach is much harder for the body to absorb compared to the heme iron found in red meat. Similarly, plant-based omega-3s are not as readily used by the body as the omega-3s found in fish.

In essence, you can get all the nutrients your body needs from animal-based foods—without the added anti-nutrients that come with vegetables. If you thrive on vegetables, great! However, for many, cutting them out could be the key to feeling better.

THE POWER OF SIMPLICITY

One of the biggest draws of the carnivore diet is its simplicity. There's no calorie counting, no complex meal plans, and no need for supplementation. You just eat meat, eggs, and animal fats until you're satisfied. This simplicity allows people to focus on nutrient-dense, bioavailable foods without worrying about fitting in the latest "superfood" or finding ways to balance macros.

The carnivore diet also removes the guessing game that comes with food sensitivities or inflammation caused by plants or processed foods. When you eliminate all plant-based foods and processed junk, you get a clearer picture of how your body responds to nutrient-rich, whole-animal foods.

Many people who switch to a carnivore diet notice that their energy levels stabilize, their digestion improves, and their mental clarity sharpens. By cutting out the noise of modern food marketing and getting back to basics, they find health in the simplicity of eating the way our ancestors did—without the confusion of today's dietary fads.

GOVERNMENT DIETARY GUIDELINES, SUCH AS THE USDA'S FOOD PYRAMID, HAVE PUSHED GRAINS AND LOW-FAT PRODUCTS.

THE REAL REASON WE'RE MISLED

One reason we've strayed so far from simple, meat-based diets is the influence of the food industry and government-backed dietary guidelines. The push for processed, low-fat, high-carb foods didn't come from an unbiased examination of human health needs. Instead, it was shaped by corporate interests, marketing, and a desire to sell products that are cheap to produce and easy to package.

For example, the rise of vegetable oils and margarine over butter was heavily influenced by industry lobbying. These processed oils are much cheaper to produce than traditional animal fats, making them more profitable for food manufacturers. However, they've also been linked to inflammation, heart disease, and other health problems.

Government dietary guidelines, such as the USDA's food pyramid, have also pushed grains and low-fat products, ignoring evidence that these foods may contribute to obesity and chronic disease. The result? A population that's more reliant on pharmaceuticals to manage preventable health conditions and a food industry that profits from our confusion about what we should eat.

It's no wonder so many people feel lost when it comes to nutrition. The carnivore diet offers a way to cut through the noise, get back to basics, and rediscover the foods our bodies are meant to thrive on.

CONCLUSION: BACK TO BASICS

At the end of the day, the carnivore diet challenges us to rethink everything we've been told about health and nutrition. By embracing nutrient-dense, animal-based foods and rejecting the overcomplicated advice that has misled us for years, we can simplify our diets and improve our health.

Is it really that crazy to think that humans might thrive on the same diet we've been eating for thousands of years? Perhaps we've strayed too far from our roots, and it's time to return to a simple, satisfying, and effective way of eating.

MANY PEOPLE WHO SWITCH TO A CARNIVORE DIET NOTICE THAT THEIR ENERGY LEVELS STABILIZE, THEIR DIGESTION IMPROVES, AND THEIR MENTAL CLARITY SHARPENS.

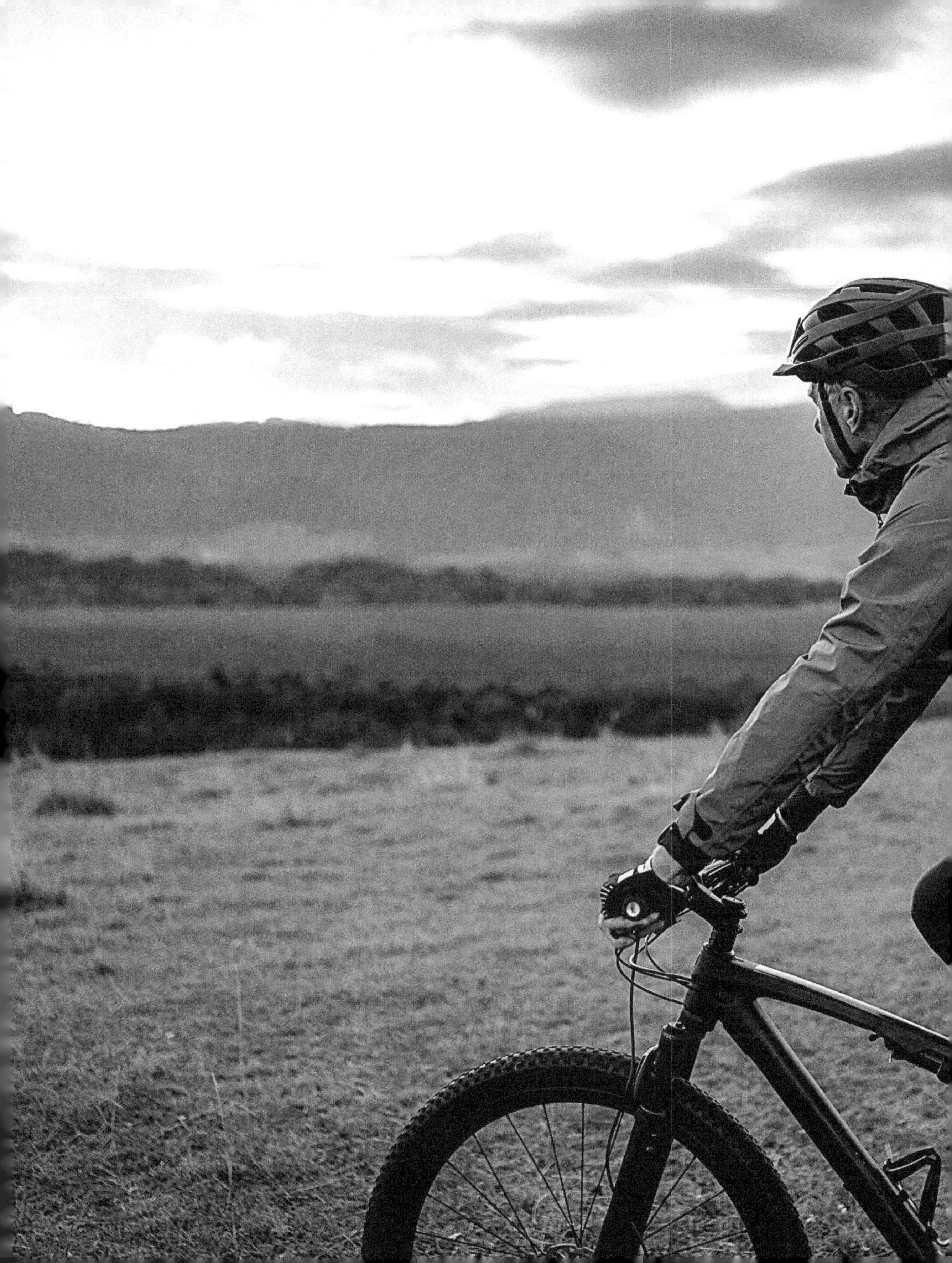

CHAPTER 2

THE NUTRITIONAL POWER OF MEAT

When it comes to nutrient-rich foods, meat stands out as a nutritional powerhouse. Packed with essential vitamins, minerals, and bioactive compounds that support our health, meat offers benefits that are difficult to replicate with plant-based diets.
In this chapter, we'll explore some of the critical nutrients found in meat—like carnosine, carnitine, creatine, taurine, zinc, vitamin B12, and heme iron—and how they contribute to overall health and well-being.

PROTEIN:
THE FOUNDATION OF HEALTH

The first thing that comes to mind when we think about meat is its rich protein content. Protein is a fundamental building block for the body, supporting muscle repair, immune function, hormone production, and much more. Meat contains all the essential amino acids our bodies need but can't produce on their own, making it a "complete protein."

However, meat's benefits go well beyond protein. While other foods provide protein, they often lack the diversity and bioavailability of other vital nutrients that meat offers. This is where meat excels as a source of nutrition contributing to optimal human health.

CARNOSINE:
THE CELLULAR PROTECTOR

Carnosine is one of the more overlooked compounds found in meat, but it plays a vital role in protecting our cells from damage. It's a dipeptide composed of two amino acids—beta-alanine and histidine—and is found mainly in muscle tissue.

CARNOSINE ACTS AS AN ANTIOXIDANT, NEUTRALIZING HARMFUL FREE RADICALS THAT CAN DAMAGE CELLS AND LEAD TO PREMATURE AGING.

Carnosine acts as an antioxidant, neutralizing harmful free radicals that can damage cells and lead to premature aging. It also helps prevent the formation of harmful advanced glycation end-products (AGEs), which are linked to chronic diseases like diabetes and cardiovascular problems. By reducing oxidative stress and glycation, carnosine supports

MEAT OFFERS BENEFITS THAT ARE DIFFICULT TO REPLICATE THROUGH PLANT-BASED DIETS

healthy aging, muscle function, and overall metabolic health.

One of the key advantages of getting carnosine from meat is that it's more readily available than from plant-based sources. Studies have shown that those who consume meat have higher levels of carnosine in their muscles, leading to better endurance, reduced muscle fatigue, and potentially enhanced cognitive function.

CARNITINE:
FUELING FAT METABOLISM

Carnitine is another nutrient found abundantly in meat. It plays an important role in energy metabolism by helping the body transport long-chain fatty acids into the mitochondria where they are burned for energy. This process supports fat metabolism and improves energy production, making carnitine particularly valuable for individuals looking to maintain a healthy weight or enhance athletic performance.

Carnitine is especially important for heart health. The heart relies heavily on fat for fuel, and carnitine helps ensure that cardiac cells efficiently utilize fatty acids. Research has shown that adequate levels of carnitine can improve cardiovascular function and may reduce the risk of heart disease.

For those who follow plant-based diets, carnitine is one of the nutrients that's difficult to obtain in sufficient amounts. While the body can produce small quantities of carnitine on its own, dietary sources from meat significantly boost levels, making it easier for your body to utilize fat as an energy source.

CREATINE:
ENHANCING STRENGTH AND COGNITIVE FUNCTION

Creatine is found almost exclusively in animal-based foods and is best known for its role in improving athletic performance. However, creatine has a wide range of health benefits that extend far beyond the gym.

Creatine is stored in muscles and acts as a quick source of energy during short bursts of intense activity such as weightlifting or sprinting. It helps regenerate adenosine triphosphate (ATP), the cell's primary energy currency. This is why creatine is so popular among athletes and bodybuilders—it enhances muscle strength, power, and endurance.

However, recent research has shown that creatine also plays a critical role in brain health. It has been shown to improve cognitive function and memory and even reduce mental fatigue, particularly in situations where the brain requires a rapid energy source. This has led to growing interest in creatine supplementation for mental health, with studies suggesting it could benefit conditions like depression and age-related cognitive decline.

TAURINE:
SUPPORTING HEART AND NERVOUS SYSTEM HEALTH

Taurine is an amino acid that's highly concentrated in meat, particularly in organ meats like liver and heart, as well as in seafood.

IN THE BODY, CREATINE IS STORED IN MUSCLES AND ACTS AS A QUICK SOURCE OF ENERGY DURING SHORT BURSTS OF INTENSE ACTIVITY.

It plays a variety of roles such as maintaining heart health, supporting the nervous system, and aiding in electrolyte balance.

Another key function of taurine is helping to regulate calcium levels within cells, which is critical for normal heart contractions and muscle function. Taurine has been shown to lower blood pressure, reduce oxidative stress, and improve blood vessel function, making it a powerful ally for cardiovascular health.

NOTE

FOR MEN

ZINC

IS IMPORTANT ······ FOR ······ TESTOSTERONE PRODUCTION & REPRODUCTIVE HEALTH

In addition, taurine is vital for brain function. It helps regulate neurotransmitters and supports healthy nerve function, contributing to improved cognitive performance and mental clarity. Studies have suggested that taurine may protect against neurodegenerative diseases and help improve symptoms of anxiety and depression.

While taurine is found in small amounts in some plant-based foods, it is far more abundant and bioavailable in animal products. Including meat in your diet ensures you're getting sufficient taurine to support both your heart and brain health.

ZINC:
A KEY MINERAL FOR IMMUNITY AND METABOLISM

Zinc is a trace mineral essential for a wide range of bodily functions, from immune support to wound healing and hormone production. Meat, especially red meat like beef and lamb, is one of the best sources of zinc, providing highly bioavailable forms that the body can easily absorb and use.

Zinc plays a crucial role in immune function, helping the body fight off infections and heal wounds. It's also involved in protein synthesis, DNA formation, and the regulation of enzymes that control metabolic processes. For men, zinc is essential for testosterone production and reproductive health.

Plant-based sources of zinc, such as legumes and grains, often contain compounds like phytates that inhibit

B12 IS ONE OF THE MOST CRITICAL NUTRIENTS FOUND ALMOST EXCLUSIVELY IN ANIMAL PRODUCTS.

zinc absorption. In contrast, the zinc found in meat is easily absorbed, ensuring you get the full benefit of this vital mineral.

VITAMIN B12:
THE ENERGY VITAMIN

Vitamin B12 is a critical nutrient found almost exclusively in animal products. It is essential for energy production, red blood cell formation, and nervous system health. Without adequate B12, the body cannot produce enough healthy red blood cells, leading to fatigue, weakness, and even neurological problems.

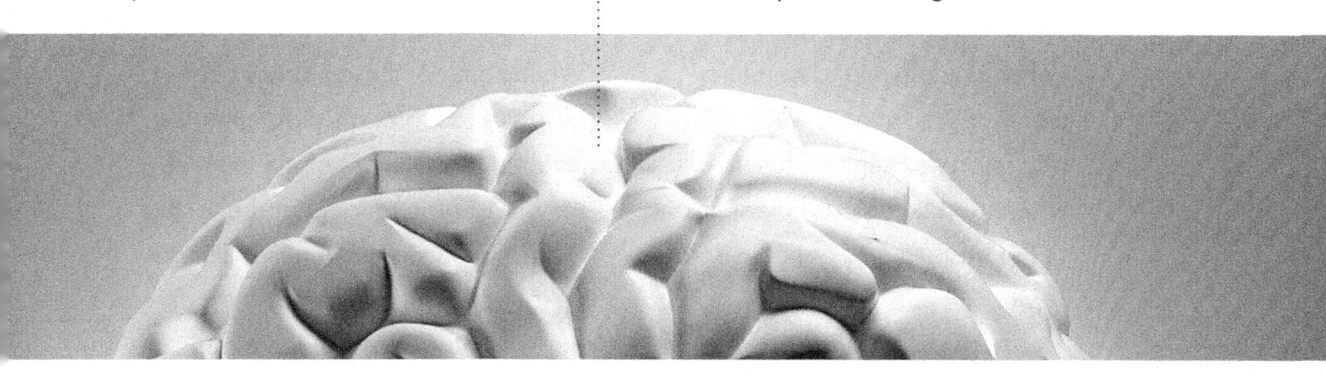

Vitamin B12 is vital for brain health. It helps maintain the myelin sheath that protects nerve fibers, and a deficiency can lead to cognitive decline, memory problems, and mood disorders. In older adults, a lack of B12 has been linked to an increased risk of dementia.

Plants do not provide a reliable source of vitamin B12. However, meat naturally contains high levels, making it the most efficient and effective way to ensure adequate intake.

HEME IRON:
THE MOST EASILY ABSORBABLE FORM OF IRON

Iron is an essential mineral that is necessary for oxygen transport in the blood, energy production, and immune function. There are two forms of dietary iron: heme and non-heme. Heme iron, found only in animal products, is much more readily absorbed by the body than the non-heme iron found in plant foods.

Heme iron helps prevent iron deficiency anemia, a condition that leads to fatigue, weakness, and impaired immune function. Meat, particularly red meat, is one of the best sources of heme iron.

CONCLUSION:
MEAT AS A NUTRITIONAL CORNERSTONE

Incorporating meat into your diet provides a wide range of essential nutrients that are difficult to obtain from plant-based sources alone. From carnosine and creatine to zinc, vitamin B12, and heme iron, the nutrients found in meat benefit many things, from muscle strength and energy production to brain function and immune health.

While some of these nutrients can be obtained through supplements or fortified foods, meat offers them in their most bioavailable and effective forms. For those looking to optimize their health, support their physical and cognitive performance, and prevent deficiencies, meat remains a valuable and irreplaceable part of a balanced diet.

FROM CARNOSINE AND CREATINE TO ZINC, VITAMIN B12, AND HEME IRON, THE NUTRIENTS FOUND IN MEAT CONTRIBUTE TO EVERYTHING FROM MUSCLE STRENGTH AND ENERGY PRODUCTION TO BRAIN FUNCTION AND IMMUNE HEALTH.

CHAPTER 3
THE ROOT PROBLEM WITH PLANTS

While plants have long been considered essential parts of a healthy diet, it is increasingly recognized that plants come with various built-in defense mechanisms, known as natural pesticides or antinutrients, that can adversely affect human health. These compounds, produced by plants to deter predators and resist environmental stressors, can interfere with nutrient absorption, digestion, and immune function in humans. For those who consume large amounts of plant-based foods, these natural pesticides may contribute to chronic health problems.

In this chapter, we will explore several key plant toxins—oxalates, lectins, glycoalkaloids, goitrogens, cyanogenic glycosides, phytic acid, protease inhibitors, flavonoids, saponins, and salicylates—discussing their potential health effects. We will also examine insights from Dr. Georgia Ede, Dr. Ken Berry, and Dr. Shawn Baker, including how populations like those in Iceland, with historically low fruit and vegetable intake, maintain robust health through animal-based diets.

OXALATES:
CRYSTALS AND KIDNEY STONES

Oxalates are naturally occurring compounds found in many plants, including spinach, beets, rhubarb, and almonds. These compounds can bind with calcium to form sharp crystals, which are difficult for the body to eliminate. When consumed in excess, oxalates can accumulate in tissues, causing a range of health problems, the most common being kidney stones.

Oxalates are also linked to joint pain and inflammation, as they can be deposited in joints and tissues, contributing to conditions like arthritis. In addition, oxalates interfere with the absorption of key minerals, particularly calcium, magnesium, and iron, leading to potential nutrient deficiencies over time.

Dr. Georgia Ede has extensively researched the dangers of oxalates and other plant compounds. She warns that modern health trends, which promote the consumption of large amounts of high-oxalate foods such as green smoothies and nut-based products, may increase the risk of oxalate-related health issues. Ede suggests that those with chronic pain, digestive issues, or recurring kidney stones may benefit from reducing or eliminating high-oxalate foods.

LECTINS:
GUT DISRUPTORS

Lectins are proteins found in many plant foods, including grains, legumes, and nightshade vegetables like tomatoes and potatoes. These compounds protect plants by binding to carbohydrates, making them indigestible to predators. However, when humans consume lectin-containing foods, these compounds can bind to the gut lining, leading to increased intestinal permeability, or "leaky gut."

This condition allows undigested food particles and toxins to enter the bloodstream, potentially triggering autoimmune reactions and inflammation. Lectins have been implicated in conditions such as rheumatoid arthritis, irritable bowel syndrome (IBS), and Crohn's disease.

Dr. Ken Berry, in his work on low-carb and carnivore diets, has emphasized the role of lectins in exacerbating autoimmune conditions and digestive issues. He argues that eliminating lectin-rich foods can significantly improve symptoms, particularly for those with chronic gut inflammation.

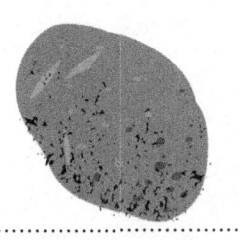

GLYCOALKALOIDS:
TOXIC NIGHTSHADES

Glycoalkaloids are toxins found in nightshade vegetables, such as potatoes, tomatoes, and eggplants. These compounds act as a natural defense mechanism against insects and other pests. In humans, glycoalkaloids can cause gastrointestinal distress, including nausea, vomiting, and diarrhea, and in high amounts may even affect neurological function.

The most well-known glycoalkaloid is solanine, which is found in potatoes, particularly in green or sprouting potatoes. While moderate consumption of nightshade vegetables is generally considered safe, individuals with sensitivities may experience chronic inflammation and worsening conditions like arthritis.

GOITROGENS:
THYROID BLOCKERS

Goitrogens are compounds found in cruciferous vegetables, such as broccoli, cauliflower, kale, and Brussels sprouts. These compounds interfere with iodine uptake by the thyroid gland, potentially leading to impaired thyroid function and the development of goiter (an enlarged thyroid). Goitrogens can be particularly harmful to individuals with preexisting thyroid conditions, such as hypothyroidism or Hashimoto's disease. While cooking can reduce goitrogen levels, large amounts of cruciferous vegetables in the diet may still affect thyroid health.

CYANOGENIC GLYCOSIDES:
HIDDEN POISONS

Cyanogenic glycosides are compounds in certain foods, including cassava, bitter almonds, and stone fruits like peaches, cherries, and apricots. When consumed, these compounds can release cyanide, a potent toxin that interferes with cellular respiration. While small amounts of cyanogenic glycosides may not pose an immediate threat, consuming improperly prepared foods like cassava can lead to cyanide poisoning, with symptoms ranging from dizziness and headache to more severe complications.

Proper preparation methods, such as soaking, fermenting, and cooking, can reduce the levels of cyanogenic glycosides in plant foods.

However, populations that rely heavily on foods like cassava, particularly in developing regions, face the risk of chronic cyanide exposure.

PHYTIC ACID:
MINERAL BLOCKER

Phytic acid, or phytate, is a compound found in the seeds of plants, including grains, legumes, and nuts. Phytic acid binds to minerals such as calcium, magnesium, iron, and zinc, preventing their absorption in the digestive tract. This anti-nutrient property can lead to mineral deficiencies, particularly in populations that rely heavily on plant-based foods as their primary source of nutrients.

Phytic acid is particularly concerning in vegetarian and vegan diets, where plant-based foods are the primary nutrition source. Even in omnivorous diets, consuming high amounts of phytic acid-rich foods can interfere with mineral absorption, leading to deficiencies in calcium and iron over time.

PROTEASE INHIBITORS:
DISRUPTING PROTEIN DIGESTION

Protease inhibitors are found in most legumes and grains, particularly soy, and in some seeds. By inhibiting the activity of proteases - enzymes responsible for breaking down proteins - these inhibitors reduce the body's ability to absorb and utilize dietary proteins.

For individuals with compromised digestive systems or those relying on plant-based proteins, protease inhibitors can exacerbate digestive issues, leading to bloating, gas, and nutrient deficiencies. Cooking and fermenting foods can reduce protease inhibitor levels, but these methods may not eliminate them entirely.

FLAVONOIDS:
ANTIOXIDANTS WITH A CATCH

Flavonoids are known for their antioxidant properties, which help neutralize free radicals and reduce oxidative stress. However, in some cases, flavonoids can act as anti-nutrients, interfering with the absorption of essential minerals like iron and calcium. High doses of flavonoids may even have pro-oxidant effects, contributing to oxidative stress rather than reducing it.

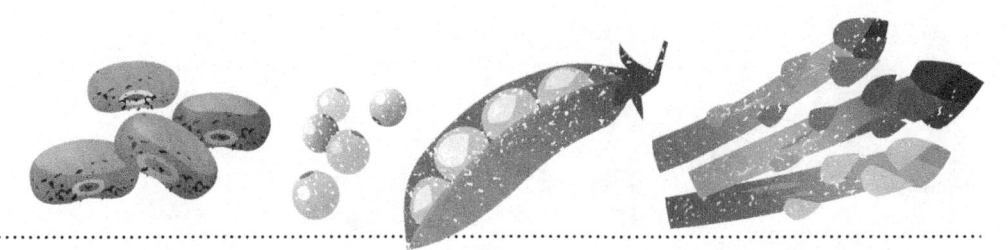

SAPONINS:
GUT IRRITANTS

Saponins are present in legumes, quinoa, alfalfa sprouts, peas, yucca and asparagus. They have been shown to interfere with the permeability of cell membranes, particularly in the gut lining, contributing to increased intestinal permeability or leaky gut. Saponins can exacerbate symptoms such as bloating, gas, and inflammation.

SALICYLATES:
SENSITIVITY REACTIONS

Salicylates are found in many fruits, vegetables, and herbs. Some individuals are sensitive to salicylates, experiencing headaches, hives, or digestive discomfort after consuming foods high in these compounds.

ICELAND

The people of Iceland have long thrived on an animal-based diet, and their health provides a great example of how humans can do well without relying heavily on fruits and vegetables. Due to Iceland's harsh climate, growing produce has historically been difficult, so the traditional diet is rich in fish, lamb, and dairy—nutrient-dense animal foods. Despite lacking plant foods, Icelanders have maintained excellent health for generations, with low rates of chronic diseases like heart disease and diabetes. Their diet, full of omega-3s from fatty fish and high-quality proteins from meat and dairy, has kept them strong and healthy, challenging the idea that fruits and vegetables are essential for good health. It's a reminder that humans can thrive on animal-based nutrition, just like the carnivore diet suggests!

CHAPTER 4

ANSWERING ALL THOSE QUESTIONS

When people first hear about the carnivore diet, it's natural for questions to be asked. After all, it's pretty much the opposite of what we've been taught for years: How can you be healthy if you're only eating meat? Let's clear up these concerns one by one.

EAT YOUR 🐄 🐖 🐑 🐟 🐔 !

WILL I GET ENOUGH VITAMINS AND MINERALS?

One of the first questions that come up is, "Aren't you missing out on essential vitamins and minerals if you don't eat fruits and vegetables?" After all, we've always heard that plant-based foods are our primary source of nutrients like vitamin C, potassium, and fiber. How do carnivores stay healthy?

First, it's important to understand that many plant nutrients are either not easily bioavailable or can be difficult for the body to use. Plants often contain antinutrients like oxalates, phytates, and lectins, which can inhibit the absorption of key minerals like magnesium, calcium, and iron. For example, the spinach on your plate may be high in iron, but much of it is bound to oxalates, so your body can't access it easily.

In contrast, the vitamins and minerals found in animal products tend to be in a more bioavailable form, meaning your body can absorb and use them more efficiently. For instance, heme iron (found in meat) is much more easily absorbed by the body than non-heme iron (from plants). Similarly, zinc, magnesium, and many B vitamins are more abundant and accessible in animal-based foods.

A common concern about the carnivore diet is whether avoiding

THE REQUIREMENT FOR VITAMIN C DROPS SIGNIFICANTLY WHEN YOU'RE NOT CONSUMING CARBOHYDRATES.

fruits and vergetable can lead to scurvy, a disease caused by vitamin C deficiency. Its important to note that the body's need for vitamin C decreases when you reduce carbohydrate intake. Vitamin C and glucose use the same pathways for absorption, so when carbohydrates are removed from the diet, less vitamin C is required for proper cellular function. Moreover, animal foods - particularly fresh, raw meats and organ meats like liver - contain small amounts of vitamin C, which can be enough to prevent deficiency in a low-carb, carnivore diet. This is why, historically, populations that relied heavily on animal-based diets, such as the inuit, did not develop scurvy, despite a lack of plant foods in their diet.

While it may seem counterintuitive, the carnivore diet provides the necessary nutrients for optimal health without relying on plant-based sources.

SHOULD I WORRY ABOUT CHOLESTEROL?

Ah, cholesterol—the eternal debate. One of the biggest fears people have about eating an all-meat diet is how it will affect their cholesterol levels and, by extension, their heart health. After all, conventional wisdom tells us that saturated fat and dietary cholesterol are the culprits behind heart disease. The truth is far more nuanced.

Let's start with cholesterol itself. Cholesterol is not inherently bad. It's a critical molecule that your body needs to function correctly. It's a component of every cell membrane, plays a crucial role in producing hormones like testosterone and estrogen, and is necessary for producing bile acids (which help digest fats).

A DIET HIGH IN ANIMAL FATS TENDS TO RAISE THE LARGE, FLUFFY LDL PARTICLES, WHICH ARE NOT ASSOCIATED WITH AN INCREASED RISK OF HEART DISEASE.

When you go carnivore and increase your intake of saturated fats and cholesterol, some people see a rise in their LDL cholesterol (often dubbed the "bad" cholesterol), which leads to panic. However, recent research has shown that the relationship between LDL cholesterol and heart disease is not as straightforward as we've been led to believe. What really matters is the type of LDL particles—whether they are small and dense (which can be harmful) or large and fluffy (which are generally benign). A diet high in animal fats tends to raise the large, fluffy LDL particles, which are not associated with an increased risk of heart disease.

Additionally, many people on the carnivore diet experience an increase in HDL cholesterol, the so-called "good" cholesterol, and a reduction in triglycerides, which are positive indicators of heart health.

Finally, it's important to note that inflammation is the actual driver of heart disease, not cholesterol itself. Numerous individuals following the carnivore diet report lower levels of systemic inflammation, which can further protect heart health. So, while it's natural to worry about cholesterol on an all-meat diet, the bigger picture points to improved heart health, not damage.

WHAT'S THE SCOOP ON POOP?

Yes, this is a legitimate concern for many people, especially given the common advice that fiber is essential for regular bowel movements. Where does the fiber come from if you're only eating

UNLIKE FIBROUS PLANT MATTER, MEAT BREAKS DOWN EFFICIENTLY IN THE DIGESTIVE SYSTEM, LEAVING LITTLE WASTE.

meat, and how does that affect your digestion?

While it's true that fiber can help bulk up stool, the idea that it's essential for digestive health has been challenged in recent years. Some people who struggle with digestive issues, such as IBS (irritable bowel syndrome), find that reducing or eliminating fiber improves their symptoms. Fiber can irritate the gut lining, leading to bloating, gas, and discomfort in certain individuals.

So, how do carnivores "poop" without fiber? The key lies in the fact that meat is highly digestible. Unlike fibrous plant matter, meat breaks down efficiently in the digestive system, leaving little waste. The result is often fewer, smaller bowel movements, but this isn't necessarily bad As long as you're not experiencing discomfort or constipation, your body is simply processing food more efficiently, with less waste to eliminate.

Many people on the carnivore diet report that their digestion improves, with less bloating, gas, and irregularity. While at first it may feel strange to have fewer bowel movements, it's usually a sign that your body is absorbing nutrients more effectively and producing less waste.

NOTE

KIDNEYS

The kidneys are incredibly efficient at processing protein

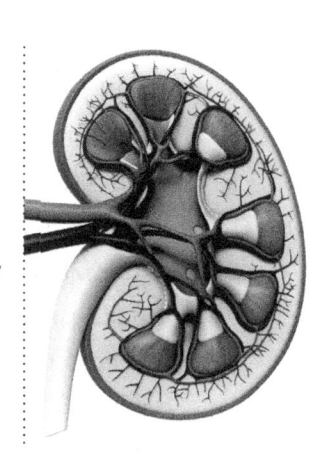

WILL THIS DIET HURT MY KIDNEYS OR CAUSE GOUT?

The idea that eating a lot of protein can "overwork" the kidneys has been around for years, but it's largely a myth when it comes to healthy individuals.

Unless you have preexisting kidney disease, there's little evidence to suggest that a high-protein diet harms kidney function. The kidneys are incredibly efficient at processing protein, and multiple studies have shown that increased protein intake doesn't damage healthy kidneys. Some research suggests that high-protein diets can help protect kidney function by maintaining muscle mass and supporting overall metabolic health.

That said, what about gout? Gout is a form of arthritis caused by elevated levels of uric acid in the blood. It can crystallize in the joints, leading to painful flare-ups. Because meat contains purines, which can raise uric acid levels, there's a perception that eating a lot of meat can cause or worsen gout. However, the relationship between purines, uric acid, and gout is more complex than "meat equals gout." Recent research suggests that it's not necessarily the purines from meat that trigger gout attacks but rather high insulin levels, poor metabolic health, and certain carbohydrates (like fructose) that increase uric acid production. Many people who adopt a carnivore diet report improved gout symptoms, likely due to improved insulin sensitivity and reduced inflammation.

In other words, a well-formulated carnivore diet helps prevent or alleviate gout, rather than cause it.

THE RELATIONSHIP BETWEEN PURINES, URIC ACID, AND GOUT IS MORE COMPLEX THAN JUST "MEAT EQUALS GOUT".

NOTE

PLANT-BASED FOODS CONTAIN NATURAL PESTICIDES AND TOXINS,

and can contribute to DNA damage and cancer risk over time.

DOES EATING ALL THAT MEAT INCREASE CANCER RISK?

The fear surrounding meat and cancer largely stems from observational studies that link high consumption of processed meats (like bacon and sausage) with an increased risk of certain cancers, particularly colorectal cancer. However, these studies don't prove that meat causes cancer—they merely show a correlation. And correlations can be influenced by many factors, including other lifestyle habits like smoking, alcohol consumption, and lack of exercise.

When it comes to fresh, unprocessed red meat, the evidence for a direct link to cancer is far less convincing. Red meat is an incredibly nutrient-dense food, providing essential vitamins, minerals, and proteins critical for maintaining good health. What's more, the carnivore diet eliminates many foods known to promote inflammation and metabolic dysfunction—two major contributors to cancer development.

Another consideration is that many plant-based foods contain natural pesticides and toxins, which can contribute to DNA damage and cancer risk over time. By cutting out these foods and focusing on nutrient-dense animal products, the carnivore diet may reduce your exposure to harmful substances.

Ultimately, cancer is influenced by many factors, including genetics, environmental exposures, and lifestyle choices. While no diet can guarantee immunity from cancer, a diet that reduces inflammation, improves metabolic health, and provides essential nutrients—like the carnivore diet—may help lower your overall risk.

CAN I STAY HEALTHY ON JUST MEAT?

The biggest question of all is, "Can you get everything your body needs from just animal products?" The short answer is yes, but let's break it down.

Animal products, especially when you include a variety of cuts and organ meats, provide all the essential nutrients your body requires. A carnivore diet covers the bases from high-quality proteins to vitamins and minerals like zinc, magnesium, iron, and B vitamins. Even omega-3 fatty acids, which we're often told come only from fish and seeds, are abundant in grass-fed meats.

Fat-soluble vitamins (A, D, E, and K) are also plentiful in animal foods. Liver, in particular, is a powerhouse of nutrition, providing massive amounts of vitamin A, as well as vitamin B12, folate, and iron. Eggs and fatty fish like salmon are excellent sources of vitamin D, while meat and dairy products supply vitamin K2.

OMEGA-3 FATTY ACIDS, WHICH WE'RE OFTEN TOLD COME ONLY FROM FISH AND SEEDS, ARE ABUNDANT IN GRASS-FED MEATS.

One important aspect of maintaining proper nutrition on the carnivore diet is variety. While steak is a favorite for many carnivores, incorporating other parts of the animal—like liver, heart, and bone marrow ensures you get a full spectrum of nutrients. These organ meats, often referred to as "nature's multivitamins," are incredibly dense in vitamins and minerals.

WHAT ABOUT LONG-TERM HEALTH ON THE CARNIVORE DIET?

There's substantial anecdotal evidence showing that people can thrive on a carnivore diet for years, even decades. Many report sustained energy, mental clarity, and the reversal of chronic health conditions like autoimmune diseases, digestive disorders, and type 2 diabetes.

While this type of evidence doesn't carry the weight of controlled clinical trials, many carnivores' personal stories highlight the potential benefits of the diet for managing chronic health issues, especially when traditional treatments have fallen short. These experiences underline the diet's potential to alleviate symptoms and restore quality of life for those who follow an animal-based nutritional diet.

Are there any risks associated with long-term carnivore eating? For most healthy individuals, the diet is sustainable and beneficial for the long haul. However, like with any diet, listening to your body is essential. Some people may find that after an initial period of health improvements, they need to adjust the balance of fat and protein or experiment with incorporating different types of animal foods to ensure they're feeling their best.

One concern some have is the potential for micronutrient deficiencies over time, especially if the diet is overly restrictive. That's why variety is vital in a carnivore diet and organ meats are such an essential part of the plan. By eating a wide variety of meats, you minimize the risk of missing out on key nutrients and can feel confident that your nutritional needs are being met.

body. However when people switch to a carnivore diet, many experience significant improvements in health markers such as blood sugar levels, insulin sensitivity, and reduced inflammation, leading to a higher quality of life.

CONCLUSION: BUSTING THE MYTHS

The carnivore diet may seem unconventional, but when you break down the common concerns, it becomes clear that many of the fears surrounding an all-meat diet are either exaggerated or based

WHEN PEOPLE SWITCH TO A CARNIVORE DIET, MANY EXPERIENCE SIGNIFICANT IMPROVEMENTS IN HEALTH MARKERS SUCH AS BLOOD SUGAR LEVELS, INSULIN SENSITIVITY, AND REDUCED INFLAMMATION

Remember, individual experimentation is important. What works for one person may not work for another; each person has to pay attention to their own

on outdated information. Concerns about vitamin and mineral deficiencies, cholesterol, digestion, kidney health, gout, cancer, and overall nutrition can be addressed through careful meal planning and understanding of how the body processes animal-based nutrients.

Animal products are nutrient-dense, but they provide these nutrients in highly bioavailable forms that the body can easily absorb and use. Whether it's the rich stores of vitamins and minerals in organ meats, the high-quality fats that promote heart and brain health, or the digestibility of meat that reduces gut inflammation, there's plenty of evidence that a carnivore diet can support long-term health and wellness.

Of course, listening to your body and adjusting as needed is always essential. For those transitioning to the carnivore lifestyle, the key is to experiment, ensure variety in your meat choices, and stay hydrated with plenty of electrolytes. The benefits of cutting out plant-based toxins and relying on animal products for nutrition are profound, as many people have discovered.

The carnivore diet is more than just a way of eating—it's a path to rediscovering how human beings can thrive when we return to a way of eating that aligns with our biological needs. So, if you've been on the fence, give it a try. The results might surprise you.

CHAPTER 5

LET FOOD HEAL YOU AND OTHER SHOCKING IDEAS

The idea that food can be used as medicine has been around for centuries, famously attributed to Hippocrates, the father of medicine. Yet, in today's world, where pharmaceutical drugs dominate the conversation around health, the notion that something as simple as your diet can prevent or reverse disease is often dismissed as "heresy." However, this idea is far from heretical; it's so important to understanding how our bodies function and how chronic diseases emerge. Nutrition plays a tremendous role in the onset and mitigation of nearly every common chronic disease and the carnivore diet may hold the key to treating some of the most pervasive health issues of our time.

CHRONIC DISEASE

When we talk about chronic diseases, we're talking about conditions that plague modern society: heart disease, diabetes, obesity, autoimmune diseases, and mental health disorders, to name a few. These diseases are often treated with a mix of medications, lifestyle changes, and occasional surgeries, but what if the root cause of many of these conditions could be traced back to something as basic as diet? For many people, a diet that emphasizes animal-based foods and eliminates plant-based irritants can not only prevent these conditions but also reverse them.

THE STANDARD AMERICAN DIET AND CHRONIC DISEASE

The Standard American Diet (SAD), which is high in processed foods, sugars, grains, and unhealthy fats, has been linked to the rise in chronic diseases. Many people's diets today are filled with chemicals, preservatives, and processed carbohydrates, all of which contribute to inflammation, insulin resistance, and nutrient deficiencies.

Inflammation is at the core of many chronic diseases. When your body is constantly inflamed—whether due to poor diet, stress, or environmental factors—it can lead to problems like heart disease, arthritis, and even cancer. Insulin resistance, driven by high carbohydrate and sugar intake, is the hallmark of type 2 diabetes.

SAD
HIGH IN PROCESSED FOODS, SUGARS, GRAINS & UNHEALTHY FATS

It is also linked to other conditions like Alzheimer's disease, which is often referred to as "type 3 diabetes." On top of this, the SAD diet is deficient in essential nutrients like high-quality fats, bioavailable protein, and fat-soluble vitamins, which are critical for cellular health, immune function, and mental well-being.

INFLAMMATION AND INSULIN RESISTANCE

The carnivore diet, by contrast, eliminates nearly all inflammatory foods. When you stop eating sugars, grains, and processed carbs, your body is no longer bombarded with foods that spike your blood sugar and cause insulin resistance. Instead, you're eating nutrient-dense, bioavailable foods—like red meat, fish, and organ meats—that support healthy blood sugar levels and reduce inflammation.

One of the ways the carnivore diet reduces inflammation is by cutting out plant compounds that can irritate the gut and contribute to chronic inflammation. For example,

THE S.A.D. DIET IS DEFICIENT IN ESSENTIAL NUTRIENTS LIKE HIGH-QUALITY FATS, BIOAVAILABLE PROTEIN, AND FAT-SOLUBLE VITAMINS

THE MOST RECOGNIZABLE USDA FOOD PYRAMID USED UNTIL 2005

NOTE

LEAKY GUT SYNDROME

WHEN THE GUT BARRIER IS COMPROMISED

lectins, oxalates, and phytates—commonly found in grains, legumes, and some vegetables—can damage the gut lining, leading to "leaky gut" syndrome. When the gut barrier is compromised, toxins and undigested food particles enter the bloodstream, triggering an immune response and chronic inflammation. By removing these plant compounds, the carnivore diet allows the gut to heal, reducing inflammation throughout the body.

AUTOIMMUNE DISEASE

Autoimmune diseases are on the rise, with conditions like rheumatoid arthritis, lupus, multiple sclerosis, and Hashimoto's thyroiditis affecting millions of people worldwide. Autoimmune diseases occur when the immune system mistakenly attacks healthy tissues in the body, often due to chronic inflammation and a leaky gut.

Many people with autoimmune diseases have found relief by eliminating foods that trigger immune responses—especially grains, legumes, and dairy.

The carnivore diet takes this further by eliminating all plant foods, which can be a game-changer for people with autoimmune conditions. When plant-based irritants are removed, many people report significant improvements in their symptoms. Dr. Baker shares countless examples of people who have seen their autoimmune diseases go into remission after adopting a carnivore diet. Whether it's eliminating joint pain from rheumatoid arthritis, reducing brain fog from lupus, or balancing thyroid function in Hashimoto's, the results are often dramatic.

CARNIVORE AND HEART DISEASE: CHALLENGING THE CHOLESTEROL MYTH

Heart disease remains the leading cause of death in many developed countries, and for decades, saturated fat and cholesterol have been blamed as the main culprits.

cholesterol particles. Large, fluffy LDL particles are relatively harmless, while small, dense LDL particles are more likely to oxidize and contribute to plaque buildup in the arteries. By reducing inflammation and improving insulin sensitivity, the carnivore diet can help shift LDL

CHOLESTEROL IS ESSENTIAL FOR THE BODY, IT'S NEEDED FOR HORMONE PRODUCTION, CELL MEMBRANE INTEGRITY, AND BRAIN FUNCTION.

The idea that eating meat—particularly red meat—raises cholesterol and leads to clogged arteries is deeply ingrained in modern nutritional advice. However, recent research challenges the long-held belief that dietary cholesterol and saturated fat are the cause of heart disease.

The real issue is inflammation and insulin resistance, not saturated fat or cholesterol. In fact, cholesterol is essential for the body—it's needed for hormone production, cell membrane integrity, and brain function. What matters most is the size and density of your LDL

particles from the harmful small, dense type to the larger, less harmful type.

Moreover, the carnivore diet is naturally low in carbohydrates, which helps regulate blood sugar and insulin levels. High insulin levels are a significant driver of heart disease as they promote inflammation and damage the lining of blood vessels. By keeping insulin levels low, the carnivore diet may reduce the risk of heart disease, even for those who consume large amounts of red meat.

MENTAL HEALTH

Conditions like anxiety, depression, and even bipolar disorder are increasingly common, and many people turn to medication to manage their symptoms. But what if diet plays a more significant role in mental health than we realize?

The brain is highly dependent on fat and protein for optimal function. Essential fatty acids, like omega-3s found in animal products, are crucial for brain health, as are amino acids, which are the building blocks of neurotransmitters. When you're eating a diet rich in animal fats and proteins, you're giving your brain the raw materials it needs to function properly.

Many people on the carnivore diet report improved mood, mental clarity, and energy levels. Some even report that they've been able to reduce or eliminate their psychiatric medications after switching to a meat-based diet. Eliminating processed foods, sugars, and plant compounds like gluten can often improve cognitive function and reduce symptoms of anxiety and depression.

THE CARNIVORE DIET AS "TREATMENT"

Given the profound impact of diet on chronic diseases, it's not a stretch to consider the carnivore diet as a form of "treatment." While this concept might be controversial in a world where pharmaceutical interventions are often the first line of defense, the idea that food can play a crucial role in healing isn't new.

ELIMINATING PROCESSED FOODS, SUGARS, AND PLANT COMPOUNDS LIKE GLUTEN CAN OFTEN IMPROVE COGNITIVE FUNCTION

THE CARNIVORE DIET ADDRESSES THE UNDERLYING FACTORS THAT CONTRIBUTE TO DISEASE: INFLAMMATION, INSULIN RESISTANCE, AND NUTRIENT DEFICIENCIES.

FOOD AS MEDICINE: A HOLISTIC APPROACH

The carnivore diet aligns with the ancient idea that food can be used as medicine. When you give your body the nutrients it needs to thrive—while eliminating foods that cause inflammation and insulin resistance—you're allowing your body to heal itself. It's important to note that the carnivore diet doesn't claim to "cure" diseases but supports the body's natural healing processes by providing a nutrient-dense, anti-inflammatory environment.

For individuals suffering from conditions like type 2 diabetes, autoimmune diseases, and obesity, the carnivore diet offers an alternative to conventional treatments. Instead of relying solely on medications that often treat the symptoms rather than the root cause, the carnivore diet addresses the underlying factors contributing to disease: inflammation, insulin resistance, and nutrient deficiencies.

CARNIVORE AS A LOW-INFLAMMATION, LOW-TOXIN DIET

The carnivore diet is inherently anti-inflammatory because it removes many foods that trigger inflammation in the body. Grains, legumes, and certain vegetables contain compounds like lectins, phytates, and oxalates that can irritate the gut and contribute to systemic inflammation. By eliminating these foods, you create a low-inflammation, low-toxin environment that allows the body to repair and heal.

In this way, the carnivore diet can

be seen as more than just a way of eating—it's a therapeutic tool that supports healing at the cellular level. Whether you're dealing with metabolic syndrome, chronic pain, or autoimmune flare-ups, the carnivore diet offers a way to manage symptoms without the need for harsh medications or invasive procedures.

imbalances, particularly insulin resistance, are at the root of obesity, and the carnivore diet offers a powerful solution.

INSULIN'S JOB IS TO HELP TRANSPORT GLUCOSE INTO CELLS FOR ENERGY, BUT WHEN RESISTANCE DEVELOPS, INSULIN LEVELS STAY ELEVATED, PROMOTING FAT STORAGE AND PREVENTING THE BODY FROM BURNING FAT FOR FUEL.

OBESITY

Obesity has become a widespread epidemic, often accompanied by chronic diseases like type 2 diabetes, heart disease, and even some cancers. Traditional advice for weight loss usually focuses on calorie restriction and exercise, but many doctors now believe that obesity is more complex than just "calories in, calories out." Instead, they emphasize that hormonal

THE ROLE OF INSULIN RESISTANCE IN OBESITY

At the heart of obesity is insulin resistance—a condition where the body becomes less responsive to insulin due to chronic exposure to high glucose levels from a carbohydrate-rich diet. Insulin's job is to help transport glucose into cells for energy. But when resistance develops, insulin levels stay elevated, promoting fat storage and preventing the body from burning fat for fuel. This hormonal imbalance makes it nearly impossible to lose weight, even on a calorie-restricted diet.

The carnivore diet targets insulin resistance by eliminating carbohydrates entirely, allowing the body to regulate insulin levels more effectively. Without the constant glucose spikes from carbs, the body shifts into a fat-burning mode, using stored fat as a primary energy source. This metabolic state, ketosis, is highly efficient for weight loss.

SATIETY AND SIMPLIFIED EATING

Unlike high-carbohydrate diets that cause blood sugar fluctuations and frequent cravings, the carnivore diet stabilizes blood sugar and promotes long-lasting fullness. In my experience, I can go for hours and not feel hungry because my meal sticks with me longer. And when I do feel hungry, I don't feel overwhelmed, shaky, or even ravenous. I simply feel hungry. This is because protein and fat from animal foods are highly satiating and keep me full for a longer period.

Additionally, the carnivore diet simplifies eating by eliminating the need to track calories or obsess over portion sizes. People eat when hungry and stop when they're full, which can lead to a more positive relationship with food. Personally, I can overeat tortilla chips all day long but it's not easy to binge on meat. I get full, and just don't want any more. Many report that their cravings for sugar and processed foods are significantly reduced or disappear altogether (which has been true in my case), making it easier to stick to the diet and achieve sustained weight loss.

INFLAMMATION AND WATER RETENTION

Chronic inflammation is another factor linked to obesity, and the Standard American Diet (SAD) is full of inflammatory foods like refined carbs and processed oils. The carnivore diet reduces inflammation by removing these foods and focusing on whole, unprocessed animal products. As a result, many people experience not only fat loss but also a significant reduction in water retention and bloating, which can contribute to a leaner appearance early in the diet.

REAL-WORLD SUCCESS

You can find thousands of success stories online about individuals who have used the carnivore diet to lose weight and reverse metabolic dysfunction. These testimonials often come from people who had previously struggled with other diets but found sustainable, long-term weight loss through the carnivore approach. Two of my favorite stories come from Kelly Hogan and Laura Spath. These ladies lost over 100 pounds each, and their testimonies of transformation are amazing! Check out the Resources Chapter on page 182 to find many more inspiring examples of success with the carnivore plan!

CONCLUSION

Obesity doesn't just involve overeating or under-exercising—it's deeply tied to hormonal imbalances, particularly insulin resistance. The carnivore diet offers a unique approach by eliminating carbohydrates, regulating insulin, and promoting fat burning. By addressing the root causes of obesity, this way of eating enables people to achieve weight loss more effectively without the stress of calorie restriction or complex diet plans. For those struggling with obesity, the carnivore diet offers a path to not just weight loss, but lasting health.

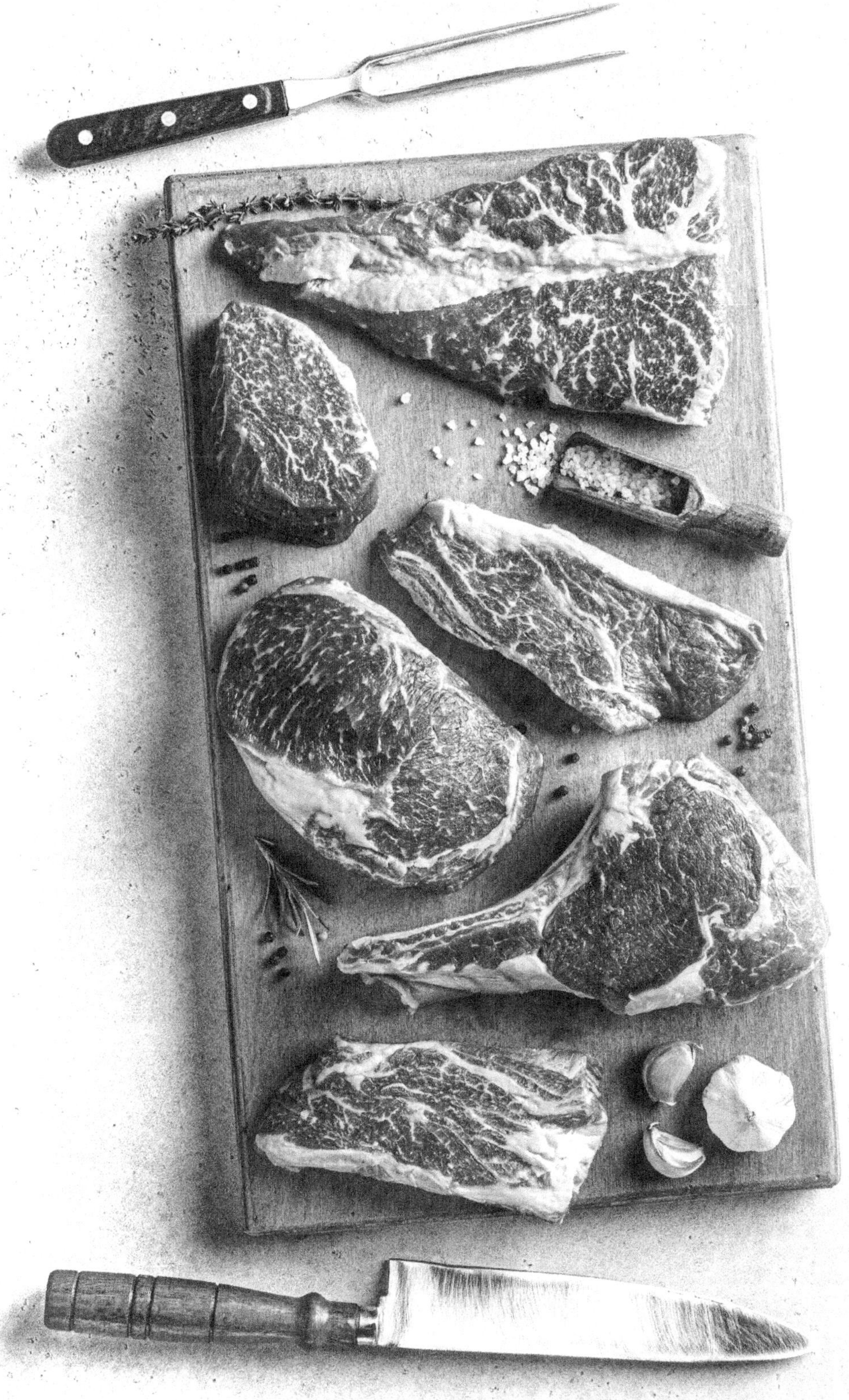

CHAPTER 6
LET'S BEGIN: TAKING THE FIRST STEPS

Embarking on a new way of eating is always exciting—and maybe a little overwhelming—but starting the carnivore diet might feel like a breath of fresh air to you. Forget all the confusing food rules, calorie counting, and endless lists of do's and don'ts. The carnivore diet strips all that away and brings it back to basics: eat meat and enjoy life.

This chapter will help you transition into the carnivore lifestyle. Whether you're ready to dive in headfirst or prefer to ease your way into it, you'll find everything you need to know to get started—from what to eat to how much to how to deal with the inevitable questions about an all-meat diet.

Let's break it down, take it step by step, and set you up for success on this delicious journey.

HOW TO GET YOUR MIND RIGHT

Switching to a carnivore diet might sound intense at first—after all, it's a complete departure from what most of us were raised on. The key to succeeding is to take it one step at a time and keep a positive mindset. The following tips will help you get started.

TAKE IT SLOW

When making any significant lifestyle change, it's easy to feel overwhelmed by the big picture.

yourself that you're trying something new that could hugely benefit your health. No pressure— just take it as it comes.

SAVOR THE JOURNEY

The carnivore diet is about abundance and simplicity. You're indulging in nutrient-dense, delicious animal foods, and that's something to enjoy! Instead of focusing on what you're giving up, think about how satisfying it is to have a meal full of steak, eggs, and butter. Your taste buds will be thanking you! I know mine did!

FOCUS ON HOW YOU FEEL TODAY, AND REMIND YOURSELF THAT YOU'RE TRYING SOMETHING NEW THAT COULD HAVE HUGE BENEFITS FOR YOUR HEALTH.

Instead of thinking about how long you'll be doing this diet or worrying about the details, take it one day at a time. Focus on how you feel today and remind

EAT UP!

One of the biggest mistakes people make when starting the carnivore diet is not eating enough. This isn't

EAT UNTIL YOU'RE SATISFIED, DON'T LEAVE THE TABLE HUNGRY.

the time to restrict calories or worry about portion sizes. Your body is adjusting, and it's important to nourish it fully. Eat until you're satisfied—don't leave the table hungry. Animal foods are incredibly satiating, and as your body adapts to burning fat for fuel, your appetite will naturally regulate itself.

AVOID THE COMPARISON TRAP

It's easy to get caught up in comparing your experience to others, especially if you're part of an online community of carnivore dieters. Remember, everyone's journey is different. Some people see changes quickly, while others take more time to adjust. What matters most is how you feel. Avoid the comparison trap and focus on your own progress.

THIS IS ABOUT YOU

When other people hear about how I am eating they are usually very curious or very skeptical, which is understandable. I mean, it does sound kinda crazy if you've never heard of it before! However, whether you're adopting this diet for weight loss, to manage chronic conditions, or just to feel better, keep in mind that you're doing this for your well-being. It doesn't matter what others think about it—this is about you and your personal goals. The carnivore diet is about reclaiming your health and feeling your best, whether others understand it or not.

HAVE FUN FEASTING

The beauty of the carnivore diet is that it celebrates abundance. Forget restrictive eating; instead, focus on feasting. Savor rich, fatty cuts of meat, indulge in eggs and bacon, and treat yourself to nutrient-dense foods like liver and bone marrow. Feasting is at the heart of this lifestyle, so don't hold back. Enjoy your meals, and let them fuel your body.

EAT MEAT

On the carnivore diet, your food list is refreshingly simple: eat meat. Let's break it down a little more so you can have a good sense of what's on the menu.

The foundation of your diet will be red meat—think steak, burgers, ground beef, ribs, and roast. These meats are packed with bioavailable nutrients like iron, zinc, and B vitamins, and they'll provide you with the fat and protein your body needs to thrive.

Other great options include poultry (chicken, turkey, duck), pork, fish, and seafood. Fatty fish like salmon and sardines are great for getting omega-3s, and seafood is a good source of minerals like iodine and selenium.

Don't forget about organ meats!

Liver, heart, and kidneys are nutrient-dense and provide vitamins and minerals that muscle meat doesn't. If you're new to organ meats, start with liver—it's a powerhouse of nutrition. (It's delicious with fried bacon!)

Eggs are also a fantastic part of the carnivore diet. They're rich in healthy fats and protein, and they're easy to prepare in countless ways. Dairy can be included as well, however, some people react to dairy so it's a good idea to remove it until health symptoms disappear. You can then reintroduce it slowly to see how your body responds.

STAY HYDRATED

Water should be your go-to beverage on the carnivore diet. Staying hydrated is important, especially as your body adjusts to a low-carb lifestyle. You can also drink coffee and tea if you like, but many people find that over time, they naturally reduce their caffeine intake because their energy levels stabilize.

Some people on the carnivore diet also enjoy bone broth, which is rich in collagen and minerals. Just be mindful of any added ingredients if you're buying it pre-made.

EAT UNTIL YOU'RE FULL

When it comes to how much you should eat, the answer is simple: eat until you're full. There's no need to track calories or measure portion sizes. Your body will naturally regulate its appetite when you're eating nutrient-dense, satisfying foods.

In the beginning, you might feel hungrier than usual as your body adjusts to this new way of eating. That's completely normal—don't be afraid to eat more than you usually would. As you settle into the diet, your appetite will stabilize, and you'll find that you naturally eat the right amount for your body.

EAT WHEN YOU'RE HUNGRY

Unlike traditional diets that recommend eating multiple small meals a day, the carnivore diet encourages you to listen to your body's hunger cues. Some people find that they feel best eating two or three larger meals a day, while others naturally gravitate toward one big meal. I sometimes eat breakfast but sometimes I skip it. I usually stop eating by 7pm. The beauty of eating carnivore is that my energy level stays constant and I feel satisfied throughout the day. No more shakes and crashes from running out of fuel. I get hungry, certainly, but I'm not crazed, desperate or hangry!

The bottomline is that, there's no one-size-fits-all answer here—just eat when you're hungry and stop when you're full. Over time, you'll figure out what meal frequency works best for you.

HOW SHOULD I PLAN MY MEALS?

A typical day on the carnivore diet might look like this:

Breakfast: A couple of fried eggs cooked in butter with a side of bacon or sausage.

Lunch: A hearty ribeye steak with some liver on the side.

Dinner: Ground beef patties or lamb chops, with a serving of bone marrow or bone broth.

Feel free to mix and match meats, eggs, and organ meats based on what you enjoy. The key is to keep it simple, satisfying, and nutrient-dense.

WHAT DOES BEING HEALTHY REALLY MEAN?

Health is often defined in terms of weight, cholesterol levels, or blood pressure. However, on the carnivore diet, we take a broader view of what health means. Health isn't just about numbers on a chart—it's about how you feel day to day. Are you energized? Do you sleep well? Is your digestion smooth and regular? Are you free of pain?

A successful carnivore diet doesn't just involve hitting a target weight or improving lab results. It means regaining control over your body, feeling vibrant, and living life to the fullest.

WHAT CHANGES WILL I NOTICE?

As with any significant dietary shift, you can expect your body to go through some changes as you transition to the carnivore diet. Some people feel amazing right from the start, while others experience a bit of an adjustment period. The key is to be patient with yourself and trust the process. Let's break down some common changes you might experience and what to expect along the way.

FATIGUE

When you first start the carnivore diet, it's not uncommon to feel a bit more tired than usual. This is often referred to as the "keto flu" or "carnivore flu," and it happens as your body shifts from relying on carbohydrates for energy to burning fat. During this transition, your energy levels might dip, but the good news is that it's temporary.

Your body is learning to become fat-adapted, meaning it's becoming more efficient at using fat for fuel instead of glucose. After pushing through this initial fatigue, many people report having more energy than they've ever experienced before. In the meantime, to help ease the transition, make sure you're staying hydrated and eating enough good fat, and by that I mean butter, ghee, lard (yes, you read that right!) and beef tallow. (I know, it's unusual!)

BATHROOM HABITS

One of the most common questions about the carnivore diet is, "What will happen to my digestion without fiber?" Your bowel movements might change, but that doesn't mean they'll become problematic. Many people find that they have fewer, smaller bowel movements on the carnivore diet. This makes sense because you're eating highly digestible, nutrient-dense food that leaves little waste behind.

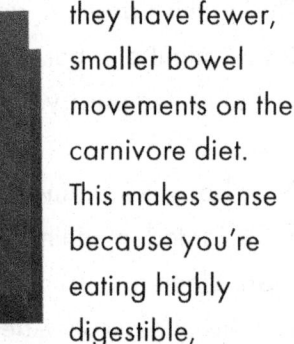

Some people may experience constipation or diarrhea during the first few weeks of the diet as their digestive system adapts, but this typically resolves on its own. Make sure to drink plenty of water and add a little extra fat to your meals if you experience constipation. On the flip side, if you're experiencing diarrhea, it might be helpful to reduce the amount of rendered fat (like melted butter or tallow) until your digestion stabilizes.

GERD AND GALLBLADDER ISSUES

If you've been struggling with acid reflux or GERD (gastroesophageal reflux disease), you may find that symptoms improve dramatically on the carnivore diet. Many people report that their acid reflux disappears within days of eliminating carbohydrates, sugars, and processed foods. The carnivore diet can help reduce inflammation and heal the gut, leading to less irritation and discomfort in the digestive tract.

If you have a history of gallbladder issues, you may also notice improvements with these. Contrary to popular belief, a diet high in healthy fats can support gallbladder function by stimulating bile release, which helps break down fat. If you've had your gallbladder removed, you can still thrive on the carnivore diet by eating smaller, more frequent meals and paying attention to how your body responds to different types of fat.

SKIN CONDITIONS

Clearer skin is another benefit many people experience on the carnivore diet. Conditions like eczema, psoriasis, and acne often improve as inflammation is reduced and the gut heals. The high intake of nutrient-dense foods like fatty meat, which provides essential vitamins like A, D, and zinc, supports skin health and helps the body repair itself from the inside out.

HEADACHES

Headaches are fairly common during the first few days or weeks of the carnivore diet, often due to dehydration or electrolyte imbalances. As your body sheds excess water weight (common when cutting carbs), you may lose electrolytes like sodium, potassium, and magnesium. Be sure to drink plenty of water and try adding a pinch of salt to your water or meals to maintain your electrolyte balance. Once your body adjusts, headaches usually disappear, and many people experience fewer headaches overall compared to their previous diets.

WHAT IF I GET MUSCLE CRAMPS?

If you experience muscle cramps on the carnivore diet, it's likely due to low electrolytes, especially magnesium or potassium. Since the diet is very low in carbohydrates, your body doesn't hold onto as much water, causing you to lose electrolytes along with it. To prevent muscle cramps, stay hydrated and focus on maintaining proper electrolyte balance. Adding salt to your meals can help you avoid these issues by replenishing lost sodium. Bone broth is another great option, as it's rich in both sodium and potassium, while seafood can help boost your magnesium levels. If you're still feeling off, you might consider supplementing with magnesium to make sure you're getting what you need. I like to take LMNT to boost my enzymes. They are powder packets that you can add to water, come in several sugar free flavors (sweetened with stevia) and are delicious! Keeping your electrolytes in check is key to staying energized and avoiding cramps while on the carnivore diet!

KETOSIS—WHAT IS IT?

Ketosis is a metabolic state where your body shifts from using carbohydrates (glucose) as its primary fuel source to burning fat for energy. This process occurs when carbohydrate intake is extremely low, prompting the liver to break down fats into molecules called ketones, which then become the body's main energy source. The carnivore diet, being high in fat and protein with few to no carbs, typically induces ketosis naturally.

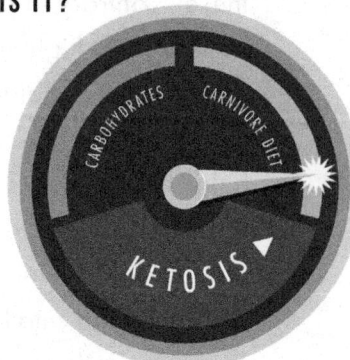

Ketosis is often credited for steady energy levels, improved mental clarity, and reduced hunger because fats and ketones provide a more consistent energy source compared to the peaks and crashes of carb-based fuel. In ketosis, your body becomes highly efficient at burning fat, making it ideal for those looking to lose weight or maintain a lean physique. As you transition into ketosis, you may experience what is known as the "keto flu," which is a temporary period where your body adapts to this new metabolic state. Symptoms can include headaches, fatigue, or irritability, but these typically subside after a few days.

Positive signs of being in ketosis include increased mental focus, stable energy throughout the day, and decreased cravings. Many people also notice that their hunger becomes more manageable, as the fat and protein from the diet keep them feeling fuller for longer periods. Unlike glucose, which causes insulin spikes, ketones

THE BRAIN RUNS EFFICIENTLY ON KETONES, AND SOME STUDIES SUGGEST THIS CAN ENHANCE COGNITIVE FUNCTION

maintain stable blood sugar levels, further contributing to appetite regulation.

Research has shown that ketosis may have therapeutic effects for neurological conditions such as epilepsy, Alzheimer's disease, and Parkinson's disease due to its neuroprotective properties. The brain runs efficiently on ketones, and some studies suggest this can enhance cognitive function, making ketosis appealing for those seeking mental clarity and focus.

CHANGE IN ENERGY LEVELS

Once you're fat-adapted, many people on the carnivore diet report a significant increase in energy. Instead of experiencing the blood sugar spikes and crashes that come with eating carbs, your energy becomes more stable throughout the day. You may find that you no longer need that afternoon nap or caffeine boost to keep going. Many carnivores say they feel more mentally alert, focused, and productive than ever before.

WHAT IS THE BEST WAY TO GET STARTED?

There are a couple of different ways to transition to the carnivore diet, depending on your starting point and how ready you feel to make the switch. Whether you're diving in headfirst or taking it slow, there's no wrong way to start—just choose the approach that works best for you.

GO ALL IN

If you're ready to fully commit to the carnivore diet from day one, this is the route for you. "Cold turkey" carnivores eliminate all plant foods immediately and focus solely on meat, fat, and animal-based products. This approach gives you a clean break from carbs and sugars and allows you to experience the full benefits of the diet quickly.

For many people, this approach results in more rapid weight loss, better mental clarity, and quicker improvements in health conditions. However, the initial adjustment period may be a little more intense, especially if you're coming from a high-carb diet.

TAKE IT EASY

If you're not quite ready to jump straight into carnivore, that's okay. A more gradual approach, where you reduce your carbohydrate intake over time, can also be effective. You might start by eliminating processed foods, grains, and sugars while still including low-carb vegetables and dairy. As you become more comfortable with the diet, you can slowly reduce your intake of plant-based foods until you're fully carnivore.

This step-down approach can help ease the transition and may result in a smoother adjustment period, especially for those who have been eating a high-carb or plant-heavy diet for a long time.

MODIFICATIONS

The carnivore diet is incredibly flexible, and there are many ways to tailor it to your individual needs. Whether you want to experiment with intermittent fasting, cycle your macronutrients, or adjust your eating habits based on your circadian rhythms, there are plenty of options to customize the diet for your lifestyle.

INTERMITTENT FASTING

Many people find that intermittent fasting naturally fits with the carnivore diet. Since animal foods are so filling and satisfying, it's not uncommon to feel less hungry throughout the day. Some people choose to eat two meals a day within a specific window (like an 8-hour window), while others prefer one large meal a day (also known as OMAD, or One Meal a Day).

Fasting can help further reduce inflammation, improve insulin sensitivity, and promote fat loss, but it's important to listen to your body and not force yourself to fast if you're feeling hungry. Fasting is a tool you can use if it feels right for you, but it's not a requirement of the carnivore diet.

CIRCADIAN BIOLOGY

Eating in line with your body's natural circadian rhythms can enhance the diet's benefits. The idea here is to align your meal times with your body's internal clock, eating during daylight hours and allowing your digestive system to rest overnight. Some people find that eating their last meal a few hours before bed improves sleep and digestion, while others feel more energized by eating larger meals earlier in the day.

MACRONUTRIENT CYCLING

Macronutrients are the essential nutrients that provide energy and are required by the body in large amounts for proper functioning; they include carbohydrates, proteins, and fats. While the carnivore diet is inherently low in carbohydrates, some people choose to cycle their protein and fat to optimize their health or fitness goals. For example, you might focus on higher protein intake on days when you're more active and shift to higher fat intake on rest days. This approach can help support muscle recovery, fat loss, and overall metabolic flexibility.

DO I NEED TO WORRY ABOUT CALORIES AND METABOLISM?

One of the great things about the carnivore diet is that it naturally regulates your hunger and energy intake. There's no need to count calories, track macros, or obsess over portion sizes. When you're eating nutrient-dense, satiating animal foods, your body will tell you when it's had enough.

However everyone's metabolism is

different. Some people may need more calories to maintain their energy levels, while others may feel best on fewer. The carnivore diet is flexible in that regard—whether you're someone with a fast metabolism who needs to eat larger portions or someone who feels satisfied with smaller meals, there's no "right" number of calories.

Many people find that their metabolism stabilizes after a few weeks or months on the carnivore diet. Since protein is highly thermogenic (meaning your body burns more calories digesting and metabolizing it), and fat is a steady source of fuel, you'll often feel more satisfied and energized without needing to constantly snack or eat large quantities.

CARNIVORE DIET OFF AND ON

You may choose to not stick to the carnivore diet 100% of the time, and that's perfectly okay. Life happens, and sometimes you'll find yourself in situations where staying strictly carnivore isn't feasible. Maybe you want to enjoy a meal with friends or have the occasional dessert. The good news is that the carnivore diet is flexible enough to accommodate these moments without derailing your overall health.

Also, the carnivore diet can be used sporadically as a reset or a way to control inflammation and improve metabolic health. Some people cycle in and out of the carnivore diet, using it as a tool to maintain optimal health while incorporating other whole foods when desired. I stick to the carnivore diet about 95% of the time, breaking it for a glass of wine or dessert with a friend. However, when I do indulge in sweets, I find that my sugar addiction flares up and I once again have to fight urges to eat a whole bag of chocolate cookies! When I remain on carnivore, I don't even feel tempted by the M&Ms or apple pie.

The key is to pay attention to how your body responds. If you feel great eating only animal products, then that's probably your ideal approach. If you feel the need to add occasional plant foods or indulge in something off-plan once in a while, that's perfectly fine too. The goal is to find what works best for you and allows you to maintain long-term health and happiness.

WHAT ABOUT MY HEALTH MARKERS?

As with any significant dietary change, it's a good idea to keep an eye on your health markers to see how your body is responding. While the carnivore diet has shown promise in improving many aspects of health, everyone's body is different, and tracking your health markers can provide valuable insights. Let's look at some key markers worth monitoring.

BLOOD LIPIDS

One of the most talked-about health markers is cholesterol, specifically LDL (low-density lipoprotein), HDL (high-density lipoprotein), and triglycerides. When switching to the carnivore diet, some people see changes in their cholesterol levels. As mentioned earlier, it's important to note that higher LDL cholesterol isn't always something to be feared—context matters. (see "cholesterol", pg 46)

Many people on the carnivore diet see improvements in their HDL-to-LDL ratio and triglyceride levels. As inflammation decreases and insulin sensitivity improves, these changes often reflect better overall cardiovascular health. However, if you have concerns about your cholesterol levels, work with a healthcare professional who understands the nuances of cholesterol and heart health.

BLOOD GLUCOSE

One of the immediate benefits of the carnivore diet is improved blood sugar regulation. Since you're cutting out all sources of sugar and carbohydrates, blood glucose levels tend to stabilize, and insulin sensitivity improves. Many people with type 2 diabetes or prediabetes see significant improvements in their glucose levels, often reducing or even eliminating the need for medication.

Monitoring your fasting blood glucose levels can help you track your progress, especially if blood sugar regulation is a primary goal for you.

LIVER FUNCTION

The liver plays a big role in fat metabolism, detoxification, and hormone regulation. It's a good idea to monitor liver function through standard blood tests, especially if you have a history of liver issues or are transitioning from a high-carb diet. For most people, the carnivore diet helps support liver health by reducing the burden of processed foods, alcohol, and sugars, but checking your liver markers can give you peace of mind.

INFLAMMATION

Chronic inflammation is a driving force behind many modern diseases, including heart disease, cancer, and autoimmune conditions. One of the reasons the carnivore diet is so effective is its ability to lower inflammation by eliminating processed foods, sugars, and inflammatory plant compounds.

You can monitor inflammation through blood tests that measure markers like C-reactive protein (CRP). Many people on the carnivore diet see a significant reduction in CRP levels, which indicates lower overall inflammation in the body.

KIDNEY FUNCTION

There's a common misconception that eating a high-protein diet is harmful to the kidneys, but research has shown that this isn't the case for healthy individuals. A diet rich in animal protein can help support kidney function by providing essential amino acids for repair and maintenance.

That said, if you have a pre-existing kidney condition, it's worth monitoring your kidney function with regular blood tests. For most people, the carnivore diet has no negative impact on kidney health, but it's always a good idea to keep an eye on things, especially if you're increasing your protein intake.

HORMONE LEVELS

The carnivore diet can have a profound impact on hormone regulation, particularly for those dealing with hormonal imbalances. By improving insulin sensitivity and reducing inflammation, the carnivore diet can help restore healthy hormone levels. This is especially true for sex hormones like testosterone and estrogen, as well as stress hormones like cortisol.

If you're transitioning to the carnivore diet with the goal of balancing your hormones, monitoring your hormone levels can provide valuable feedback on your progress.

IRON LEVELS

Red meat is an excellent source of bioavailable iron, and many people who follow the carnivore diet see improvements in their iron levels, especially if they were previously anemic. Do monitor your iron levels, particularly if you're prone to low iron or have been diagnosed with anemia in the past.

On the other hand, if you're someone who tends to store too much iron (such as in conditions like hemochromatosis), keeping an eye on your iron markers is important to ensure your levels stay within a healthy range.

MISCELLANEOUS HEALTH MARKERS

There are other health markers you might want to monitor, depending on your specific health concerns. These can include things like thyroid function, vitamin D levels, and bone health markers. Since the carnivore diet is rich in nutrients, many people see improvements in these areas, but regular check-ups and blood tests can help you stay on track and catch any potential issues early.

IS CARNIVORE SAFE FOR EVERYONE?

The carnivore diet is remarkably versatile and can be beneficial for a wide range of people, but like any dietary approach, it's not a one-size-fits-all solution. Here's a breakdown of who the carnivore diet is generally safe for and a few considerations to keep in mind.

AUTOIMMUNE CONDITIONS

Many people with autoimmune diseases, such as rheumatoid arthritis, lupus, and Hashimoto's thyroiditis, have found relief from their symptoms on the carnivore diet. By eliminating plant foods that contain lectins, oxalates, and other inflammatory compounds, the carnivore diet helps reduce the burden on the immune system, allowing the body to heal.

METABOLIC ISSUES

Those with metabolic conditions like type 2 diabetes, insulin resistance, and obesity often see significant improvements on the carnivore diet. By removing processed carbohydrates and sugars, the diet helps regulate blood sugar and insulin levels, making it easier to lose weight and manage metabolic health.

MENTAL CLARITY

People frequently find that the carnivore diet enhances mental clarity, focus, and mood. By eliminating processed foods, sugars, and grains, which can contribute to brain fog and mood swings, the carnivore diet provides a steady source of energy that keeps the brain functioning at its best.

PREGNANT & BREASTFEEDING WOMEN

While the carnivore diet can provide the essential nutrients needed during pregnancy and breastfeeding, it's important to make sure you're eating enough calories and a variety of nutrient-dense animal foods. Pregnant and breastfeeding women should work with a healthcare provider to ensure they're getting adequate nutrition for both themselves and their babies.

CHILDREN

The carnivore diet can also be a healthy option for children. Dr. Ken Berry, a board-certified family physician and well-known advocate of the carnivore diet, suggests that a properly implemented carnivore diet can be safe for children when done thoughtfully and with proper guidance. He emphasizes the importance of including nutrient-dense animal products that provide essential vitamins and minerals for growth and development. Berry advocates for a diet that eliminates processed sugars and grains, which he argues are more harmful to long-term health, and highlights how whole, unprocessed animal foods can provide the nutrition children need for optimal health.

ISN'T THERE AN ALL-MEAT DIET CONTROVERSY?

There's no denying that the carnivore diet has stirred up controversy, especially among those who advocate for plant-based diets. Let's address some of the common concerns and myths surrounding an all-meat diet:

ORGAN MEATS

Organ meats, such as liver, heart, and kidneys are some of the most nutrient-dense foods on the planet. They provide essential vitamins and minerals that are often lacking in muscle meat alone. While some people may feel squeamish about eating organ meats, incorporating them into your diet can help you achieve optimal health.

If you're new to organ meats, start with liver, which is packed with vitamin A, iron, and B vitamins. You don't need to eat large amounts—a small serving a couple of times a week can provide significant health benefits.

RAW MEAT

Some carnivores choose to include raw meat in their diet, but it's important to exercise caution if you decide to go this route. While raw meat can be rich in nutrients and enzymes, it also carries a higher risk of bacterial contamination. If you're interested in experimenting with raw meat, make sure to source it from high-quality, reputable sources and handle it with care.

GRASS-FINISHED BEEF

There's a lot of debate about whether grass-finished beef is superior to grain-finished beef. True, grass-finished beef does have a higher omega-3 content and more vitamins like vitamin E, however, both grass-finished and grain-finished beef are excellent sources of protein, fat, and essential nutrients. If you have access to grass-finished beef and prefer the taste, go for it. However, if it's not readily available or within your budget, grain-finished beef is still a fantastic option.

HOW DO I COOK MY FOOD THE CARNIVORE WAY?

When it comes to cooking on the carnivore diet, simplicity is key. The natural flavors of meat often shine through without the need for elaborate cooking techniques or a long list of ingredients. The diet may seem restrictive at first glance, but there is a variety of ways to prepare your meals that keep things interesting without adding complexity.

Grilling, pan-searing, slow-cooking, and even air frying are popular methods that bring out the best in different cuts of meat. A cast-iron skillet can be your best friend when it comes to cooking steaks, burgers, or liver. The high heat and even heat distribution of the cast iron ensures a perfect sear, locking in the juices and creating that delicious crust on the outside. I have a chicken thighs recipe that calls for a cast iron skillet. That chicken not only cooks fast, it tastes fabulous! (see pg 160)

YOU CAN OPT FOR STEAKHOUSES OR BBQ JOINTS OR EVEN BREAKFAST DINERS FOR BACON & EGGS.

For larger cuts like pork shoulder or brisket, slow cooking or using a pressure cooker can deliver tender, fall-apart meat with minimal effort. Throw the meat in with some salt and let it cook for several hours, and you'll have a meal that's not only delicious but also ideal for meal prep throughout the week.

Roasting meats in the oven is another fantastic option. Whether it's chicken thighs, pork belly, or a whole roast, a little bit of salt and some time in the oven is often all you need for a flavorful meal. Experiment with different cooking methods to keep things interesting and find what works best for you.

WHAT ABOUT WHEN I TRAVEL?

Traveling on the carnivore diet might sound like a challenge, but with a little preparation, it's entirely manageable. Whether you're hitting the road for a family vacation or flying across the country for work, there are ways to stay carnivore-compliant without stress.

First, let's talk about road trips. Aside from the fact that I LOVE them, packing a cooler with carnivore-friendly snacks makes traveling a breeze. Think boiled eggs, slices of steak, jerky (make sure it's sugar-free), or cooked ground beef patties. You can even pre-cook and freeze meals ahead of time, so they stay fresh during your trip and are ready to eat whenever you are. If you're staying in a hotel, bringing an electric skillet or a small portable grill can allow you to cook your own meals easily.

When flying, things get a little trickier, but not impossible. Hard-boiled eggs, cheese, and jerky are all airport-friendly snacks.

Starbucks, found at most airports, offers egg bites and coffee with heavy cream. Once you arrive at your destination, a quick grocery store stop can set you up with the basics like ground beef, steaks, or rotisserie chicken. Many hotels now have mini-fridges and microwaves, which allow for basic meal prep.

Dining out while traveling is usually not a problem. I can almost always find something carnivore on any restaurant menu. You can opt for steakhouses, barbecue joints or even breakfast diners for bacon and eggs. Order your beef or fish grilled and your burgers without the bun.

Most restaurants are accommodating if you ask for a no-frills, meat-only plate, and don't be afraid to request butter on the side for some added fat. Even if you find yourself at McDonald's, you can still opt for several meat patties in a container, which is a better choice than grabbing pizza or fried chicken. I've done that many times in a pinch and its very satisfying! With these strategies, you can stick to the carnivore diet no matter where your travels take you.

CHAPTER 7

REAL LIFE CARNIVORE JOURNEYS

HOW THE CARNIVORE DIET TRANSFORMS LIVES

The carnivore diet, with its focus on nutrient-dense animal foods and complete elimination of plant-based products, has gained significant popularity for its ability to bring about life-changing health benefits. Whether it's overcoming autoimmune diseases, achieving sustainable weight loss, or eliminating chronic health issues, thousands have found success by adopting this meat-based lifestyle. Here, we read the personal journeys of nine individuals who took control of their health and experienced remarkable transformations by following the carnivore diet.

KELLY HOGAN:
FROM LIFELONG OBESITY TO OPTIMAL HEALTH

Kelly Hogan's struggle with obesity began in her childhood and continued into adulthood. Despite her best efforts to follow mainstream diet advice—counting calories, exercising excessively, and cutting fat—she could not lose weight. As she grew older, the frustration of yo-yo dieting took its toll on her mentally and physically. She followed mainstream advice to eat more fruits, vegetables, and whole grains, but her weight remained a constant problem.

In 2009, Kelly discovered the zero-carb carnivore lifestyle. With skepticism but a willingness to try anything, she began eliminating all plant foods from her diet and focused solely on eating animal-based products like beef, eggs, and butter. The results were nothing short of miraculous. In just a few months, Kelly shed over 100 pounds, and for the first time in her life, she could maintain a healthy weight without hunger or cravings. Along with the weight loss came improved energy, relief from chronic joint pain, and a sense of well-being that she had never experienced before.

More than a decade later, Kelly has maintained her weight loss and continues to thrive on the carnivore diet. She has become an advocate for the lifestyle, sharing her story and helping others find the same success. Her journey serves as a testament to the power of simplicity in nutrition and how eliminating processed foods and carbohydrates can lead to long-term health improvements. Today, Kelly is a vibrant, energetic mother of three,

> **FOR THE FIRST TIME IN HER LIFE, SHE WAS ABLE TO MAINTAIN A HEALTHY WEIGHT WITHOUT HUNGER OR CRAVINGS.**

NOTE

KELLY SHED **OVER 100 POUNDS** IN A FEW MONTHS

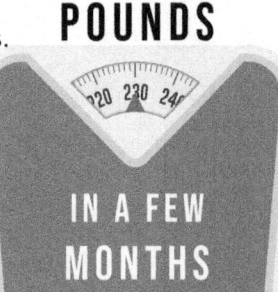

NOTE

BEEF SALT AND WATER ONLY!

MIKHAILA PETERSON: OVERCOMING AUTOIMMUNE DISORDERS AND DEPRESSION

and her story continues to inspire countless individuals struggling with weight and health challenges.

Mikhaila Peterson's story is one of perseverance and determination in the face of debilitating health challenges. From a young age, Mikhaila suffered from a host of autoimmune issues, including juvenile rheumatoid arthritis, which led to multiple joint replacement surgeries by the time she was a teenager. On top of that, she battled severe depression, anxiety, and chronic fatigue. Her health continued to deteriorate despite numerous medical interventions, medications, and dietary changes. By her early twenties, Mikhaila was struggling just to function day to day.

In 2015, after trying every conceivable diet and treatment, Mikhaila decided to try something drastic: the carnivore diet. She eliminated all plant-based foods from her diet and began eating only beef, salt, and water. The results were life-changing. Within weeks, her inflammation reduced, her joint pain subsided, and her mental health improved dramatically. Over time, she was able to wean herself off her medications and found a level of stability and energy she had never experienced before.

Mikhaila credits the carnivore diet for saving her life and giving her a future she never thought possible. Her story has since garnered worldwide attention, and she has become a prominent figure in the carnivore and autoimmune communities. Through her blog, social media presence, and public speaking, Mikhaila shares her journey and helps others facing similar struggles. Her success serves as a beacon of hope for those suffering from chronic illness, proving that a simple diet focused on nutrient-dense animal foods can yield profound results.

JOE & CHARLENE ANDERSON:
THRIVING ON TWO DECADES OF CARNIVORE

> **NOTE**
>
> JOE & CHARLENE ANDERSON
>
> CARNIVORE FOR MORE THAN
>
> **20**
>
> **YEARS**

Joe and Charlene Anderson are two of the longest-standing proponents of the carnivore diet, having followed it for more than 20 years. Their journey began when Charlene was battling chronic fatigue, digestive issues, and skin problems that no doctor or treatment could resolve. Joe, though healthy, joined her in exploring dietary changes to support her healing. After experimenting with various low-carb and ketogenic approaches, they decided to try a carnivore diet, eliminating all plant foods and focusing exclusively on animal products like beef, lamb, and eggs.

The results were transformative for both of them. Charlene's chronic fatigue lifted, her digestive problems disappeared, and her skin cleared up. She regained her energy and vitality, and Joe experienced unexpected benefits, including increased mental clarity, sustained energy, and a noticeable improvement in his physical performance. The Andersons have thrived on the carnivore diet for over two decades and have come to rely on its simplicity and effectiveness to maintain their health and well-being.

Their success has made them pillars of the carnivore community, where they actively share their experiences and offer guidance to others who are curious about the diet. Joe and Charlene's long-term commitment to carnivory proves that a meat-based diet can be a sustainable way of eating that provides lasting health benefits. They continue to inspire others with their story, showing that it's possible to enjoy excellent health well into the later stages of life by returning to a natural, ancestral way of eating.

DR. SHAWN BAKER:
LEADING THE CHARGE FOR CARNIVORE NUTRITION

Dr. Shawn Baker, an orthopedic surgeon, is one of the most well-known advocates of the carnivore diet. A lifelong athlete and health enthusiast, Dr. Baker had always been in great shape, but as he got older, he began noticing a decline in his performance and recovery. Despite following a high-protein, low-carb diet, he was dealing with nagging joint pain, inflammation, and reduced stamina. His search for a solution led him to the carnivore diet.

In 2016, Dr. Baker decided to try eating only meat and animal products, cutting out all plant-based foods. To his surprise, the results were almost immediate. His joint pain disappeared, his energy levels soared, and he recovered faster and performed better than ever in his athletic pursuits. At 50, Dr. Baker was setting world records in rowing and outperforming athletes half his age. His success on the carnivore diet didn't just improve his physical health—it also enhanced his mental clarity and overall sense of well-being.

Dr. Baker's personal experience with the carnivore diet led him to become one of its leading advocates. He published *The Carnivore Diet*, where he shares his journey and the science behind why this diet works for so many people. His online platform, Revero, is a community hub where people from around the world share their success stories and receive support for adopting an animal-based diet. Dr. Baker continues to educate the public about the health benefits of carnivory, advocating for its use for optimizing human health.

DANNY VEGA:
FROM KETO SUCCESS TO CARNIVORE PEAK PERFORMANCE

Danny Vega, a former collegiate athlete and powerlifter, had already found success with the ketogenic diet when he decided to take his nutrition a step further. A staunch advocate for low-carb living, Danny had experienced fat loss, improved energy, and enhanced physical performance on keto. However, he wanted to see if he could push his fitness and health to the next level. That's when he discovered the carnivore diet.

In 2017, Danny transitioned from keto to carnivore, cutting out the small number of plant-based foods he was still consuming. The impact on his performance was undeniable—his energy levels shot through the roof, his recovery times shortened, and he gained lean muscle mass more easily. Danny also noticed that his cognitive function improved, allowing him to focus better both in and out of the gym.

BELLA DECIDED TO TRY THE DIET, WHICH CONSISTS ENTIRELY OF ANIMAL-BASED FOODS LIKE MEAT, EGGS, AND DAIRY.

Now, as a dedicated carnivore, Danny uses his platform to educate others about the benefits of a meat-based diet for athletic performance and overall health. Through his podcast Fat Fueled Family, he shares his experiences and coaches individuals on how to optimize their nutrition for peak

WITHIN WEEKS OF ADOPTING THE DIET, HE NOTICED IMPROVEMENTS IN HIS ENERGY LEVELS, MENTAL CLARITY, AND DENTAL HEALTH.

performance. Danny's journey is a testament to how the carnivore diet can take fitness and health to the next level, especially for athletes looking for an edge.

BELLA:
THE STEAK & BUTTER GAL:
REVERSING SEVERE ECZEMA AND CHRONIC FATIGUE.

Bella, also known as the Steak and Butter Gal, faced a variety of health struggles before adopting the carnivore diet. Her issues included severe eczema, digestive problems, and continual fatigue. These conditions left her feeling frustrated and disheartened as she tried multiple diets, including veganism, to find relief. However, none of these approaches seemed to address her core health concerns. She was left trapped in a cycle of discomfort and low energy.

In 2019, Bella discovered the carnivore diet through various online communities and testimonies from others who had seen significant health improvements. Skeptical at first, Bella decided to try the diet. Within weeks, she began to see dramatic improvements in her eczema, digestion, and energy levels. Her skin cleared up, and she felt more energized and mentally sharp than she had in years.

Bella's success with the carnivore diet inspired her to share her journey through social media, where she built a large following. She now uses her platform to educate others about the benefits of a carnivore lifestyle and provides support to those struggling with similar health issues. Bella's journey is a testament to how a dietary shift can transform one's physical and mental well-being.

KEVIN STOCK:
DENTAL HEALTH AND ENERGY BOOST

Dr. Kevin Stock, a dentist and health advocate, has always been interested in nutrition and fitness. After experimenting with various diets, including ketogenic and paleo approaches, he decided to try the carnivore diet to optimize his health and dental well-being.

Dr. Stock was initially drawn to the carnivore diet because of its simplicity and focus on nutrient-dense foods. Within weeks of adopting the diet, he noticed improved energy levels, mental clarity, and dental health. His gums became healthier, and he experienced fewer cavities—which he attributed to eliminating sugars and plant-based foods that can contribute to tooth decay.

Dr. Stock continues to follow and promote the carnivore diet, sharing his insights on its benefits for overall health and well-being through his blog and interviews.

NOTE

MIGRAINE FREE AFTER 15 YEARS

TARA:
RECOVERY FROM CHRONIC MIGRAINES

Tara had suffered from severe migraines for over 15 years, trying various treatments from medications to alternative therapies, yet nothing provided consistent relief. Her migraines were often so debilitating that they left her bedridden for days, negatively affecting both her professional and personal life. Desperate for a solution, Tara decided to try the carnivore diet after hearing about others' positive experiences. To her surprise, within a few weeks, the frequency and intensity of her migraines began to decrease. The inflammation that had been triggering her headaches diminished, allowing her to stop relying on medication. Today, Tara remains migraine-free, stating, "I never thought I would live without migraines. The carnivore diet gave me my life back."

DR. KEN BERRY:
WITNESS TO THOUSANDS OF TRANSFORMED LIVES

Dr. Ken Berry, a board-certified family physician, initially approached the carnivore diet with skepticism. Like many in the medical field, he had been trained to promote a balanced diet rich in fruits, vegetables, and whole grains. However, after witnessing many of his patients struggle with obesity, diabetes, and other chronic conditions despite following these recommendations, he began to question conventional nutritional wisdom.

Through personal experimentation, Dr. Berry found that low-carb and ketogenic diets improved his health. Still it wasn't until he adopted a strict carnivore diet that he saw profound changes. Struggling with joint pain, weight issues, and autoimmune symptoms, Dr. Berry experienced remarkable improvements in his energy levels, mental clarity, and physical well-being. Even his chronic skin condition, his rosacea, dramatically improved on the carnivore diet.

As he investigated the science behind the carnivore lifestyle, Dr. Berry became convinced that many of the health problems people face are linked to plant toxins and poorly absorbed nutrients in plant-based foods. He emphasizes the bioavailability of nutrients from animal products, like heme iron and B12, and the reduction of inflammation by eliminating plants.

These days, Dr. Berry is a vocal advocate for the carnivore diet, sharing countless patient success stories through his YouTube channel and social media. From improved blood sugar control to relief from autoimmune disorders, he has witnessed how an all-meat diet can transform lives. His personal and professional journey serves as an inspiring testament to the potential benefits of carnivore eating.

DR. BERRY BECAME CONVINCED THAT MANY OF THE HEALTH PROBLEMS PEOPLE FACE ARE LINKED TO PLANT TOXINS AND POORLY ABSORBED NUTRIENTS

CHAPTER

8

HOW VEGANISM FALLS SHORT

THE PRESSURE TO EAT PLANTS

The movement toward plant-based diets has gained immense momentum in recent years. Health organizations, mainstream media, and even governments have recommended that we shift toward consuming more plants and less meat. They argue that plant-based diets reduce the risk of heart disease, diabetes, cancer, and other chronic diseases. For many people, this has led to the belief that veganism is the key to long-term health and longevity.

Dr. Paul Saladino, one of the most well-known advocates of the carnivore diet, disagrees. In his book The Carnivore Code, he highlights the nutritional inadequacies of a plant-only diet, stating, "Plants are survival foods, not optimal foods for humans." Saladino explains that while plants can provide some nutrients, they also contain anti-nutrients like oxalates, lectins, and phytates, which can interfere with nutrient absorption and contribute to inflammation.

One of the significant problems with plant-based diets is that they often lead to deficiencies in crucial vitamins and minerals. While vegans can get some nutrients from plants, others—like vitamin B12, heme iron, and DHA omega-3s—are only found in animal foods in their most bioavailable forms. This is why many long-term vegans develop health issues like anemia, fatigue, and neurological problems if they don't supplement correctly.

Frank Tufano, a popular carnivore advocate on YouTube, discusses the toll a vegan diet took on his health before switching to carnivore. "After being vegan for over seven years, I started experiencing constant fatigue, digestive issues, and chronic anxiety. It wasn't until I reintroduced meat that my health began to improve." Another notable example of someone who transitioned from a vegan to a carnivore diet is Alyse Parker, a YouTuber and lifestyle influencer. Alyse followed a vegan diet for over four years but began to experience declining health, including digestive problems, low energy, and food sensitivities. In 2019, she decided to try the carnivore diet as an experiment.

"AFTER BEING VEGAN FOR OVER SEVEN YEARS, I STARTED EXPERIENCING CONSTANT FATIGUE, DIGESTIVE ISSUES, AND CHRONIC ANXIETY."

NOTE

WITHIN 30 DAYS

Alyse reported feeling more energized and free from many of the issues she faced on a vegan diet.

Within 30 days, she reported feeling more energized and free from many of the issues she'd faced on a vegan diet. Many former vegans like Frank and Alyse have shared similar stories, where their health began to deteriorate after several years of avoiding animal products, leading them to reintroduce meat for optimal nutrition.

Dr. Ken Berry, another carnivore proponent and author of *Lies My Doctor Told Me*, highlights the importance of animal products for overall health. "Human beings have been thriving on animal-based diets for millions of years. It's no coincidence that when people adopt these traditional diets, they see improvements in their health markers, from cholesterol to blood pressure."

While there's no denying that some people experience short-term benefits on plant-based diets—often due to the elimination of processed junk food—many find that they develop nutrient deficiencies or other health issues over time. According to carnivore advocates, the long-term sustainability of a plant-only diet is, questionable at best.

ENVIRONMENTAL CONCERNS: WHAT'S REALLY HAPPENING?

One of the key arguments in favor of veganism is that it's better for the environment. Vegans claim that animal agriculture is a major contributor to climate change, deforestation, and water usage. Popular documentaries like Cowspiracy argue that if we want to save the planet, we must stop eating meat.

VEGANS CLAIM THAT ANIMAL AGRICULTURE IS A MAJOR CONTRIBUTOR TO CLIMATE CHANGE, DEFORESTATION, AND WATER USAGE.

106

However, the environmental impact of animal farming isn't as clear-cut as vegan advocates would have you believe. Dr. Peter Ballerstedt, a leading voice in the regenerative agriculture movement, argues that well-managed animal farming can benefit the environment. "Grazing animals are a crucial part of the ecosystem. They promote soil health, sequester carbon, and increase biodiversity." According to Ballerstedt, it's not the animals themselves that are the problem— it's the industrial farming practices that harm the planet.

Regenerative agriculture, a system that mimics natural ecosystems by rotating animals on pastures, can improve the land. The animals graze on grass, fertilize the soil, and allow plant life to regenerate. This system reduces carbon emissions and can restore degraded land and enhance biodiversity.

IT'S NOT THE ANIMALS THEMSELVES THAT ARE THE PROBLEM, IT'S THE INDUSTRIAL FARMING PRACTICES THAT HARM THE PLANET.

CROPS LIKE SOY, WHEAT, AND CORN REQUIRE VAST AMOUNTS OF LAND, WATER, AND CHEMICAL INPUTS LIKE PESTICIDES AND FERTILIZERS.

On the flip side, large-scale monocrop agriculture, which is necessary to support a global plant-based diet, has its own environmental drawbacks. Crops like soy, wheat, and corn require vast amounts of land, water, and chemical inputs like pesticides and fertilizers. This type of farming leads to soil depletion, water pollution, and the destruction of natural habitats.

Joel Salatin, a well-known advocate of regenerative farming, has spoken extensively about the environmental impact of industrial agriculture. He points out that mono-crop farming destroys the ecosystems it claims to save. "You can't have a regenerative farm without animals," he says. "They're the heartbeat of the land, and when we remove them, we disrupt nature's cycle."

Water usage is another point of contention in the vegan-versus-carnivore debate. While it's often claimed that raising livestock uses more water than growing crops, this argument is based on flawed data. Many environmental assessments don't account for the fact that much of the water used in livestock farming is rainfall on pastureland, which would occur regardless of whether animals were raised there or not. In contrast, water-intensive crops like almonds and rice are grown in areas where water resources are already scarce.

The carnivore perspective argues that a diet focused on sustainably raised, grass-fed animals is healthy for humans and can be environmentally friendly when done correctly. A 2018 study published in *Frontiers in Sustainable Food Systems* concluded that regenerative grazing practices could sequester more carbon in the soil than industrial animal farming produces, making well-managed livestock farming a net-positive for the environment.

ETHICAL AND REGENERATIVE FARMING PRACTICES ALLOW ANIMALS TO LIVE IN NATURAL CONDITIONS, WITH ACCESS TO PASTURE, SUNLIGHT, AND SPACE TO ROAM.

THE TRUTH ABOUT ANIMAL WELFARE AND SUSTAINABILITY

Another central argument for veganism is the idea that eating animals is inherently unethical. Factory farming conditions, where animals are confined to small spaces, fed unnatural diets, and subjected to harsh conditions, are undeniably cruel. For many people, the moral implications of this system are reason enough to stop consuming animal products altogether.

However, as carnivore advocates point out, not all animal farming operates this way. Ethical and regenerative farming practices allow animals to live in natural conditions, with access to pasture, sunlight, and space to roam. These animals are not raised in confinement but are part of a balanced ecosystem that includes land regeneration and biodiversity.

Dr. Anthony Chaffee, a former professional rugby player turned carnivore advocate, emphasizes the importance of supporting ethical, humane animal farming. "We've been misled to believe that all animal farming is factory farming, but that's not true. Regenerative farms allow animals to live naturally, and in doing so, they're contributing to the health of the soil and the environment."

One of the most overlooked aspects of plant-based farming is the unintended harm caused by monocrop agriculture. As Joel Salatin points out, "Mono-cropping leads to the death of countless small animals—mice, rabbits, birds, and insects—all of whom are killed in the process of plowing fields, spraying pesticides, and harvesting crops." While these deaths may not be as visible as the slaughter of livestock, they are no less real.

Veganism also doesn't account for animals' essential role in regenerating soil. By eliminating animals from our food system, we risk further degrading the land through industrial crop farming, which relies on synthetic fertilizers and pesticides. Dr. Baker emphasizes that ethical carnivores support small-scale, regenerative farms where animals are treated with respect throughout their lives and play a vital role in maintaining healthy ecosystems.

WE RISK FURTHER DEGRADING THE LAND THROUGH INDUSTRIAL CROP FARMING, WHICH RELIES ON SYNTHETIC FERTILIZERS AND PESTICIDES.

Life and death are inseparable, whether we're talking about plants or animals. By supporting regenerative agriculture, we can respect animals while contributing to a healthier planet. carbon, improve soil, and boost biodiversity. In contrast, mono-crop agriculture depletes soil and harms ecosystems, showing that plant farming isn't always "green."

THE GOAL SHOULDN'T BE ELIMINATING ANIMAL PRODUCTS BUT SUPPORTING FARMS THAT RAISE ANIMALS HUMANELY.

SUMMING UP THE VEGAN DEBATE

Health Benefits: Many people initially feel better on plant-based diets, not because they eliminate animal products, but because they cut out processed junk food. However, long-term vegans often face nutrient deficiencies in essentials like vitamin B12, iron, and DHA, which are only abundant in animal foods.

Environmental Impact: While industrial farming is harmful, regenerative farming can sequester

Animal Cruelty: The goal shouldn't be to eliminate animal products but to support farms that raise animals humanely. Mono-crop farming kills countless small animals, insects and birds in the process of growing crops for human consumption. Ethical carnivores promote humane, regenerative practices that respect the natural cycle.

Moral Superiority: Veganism is often considered superior, but life and death are natural. The carnivore approach encourages

WHILE VEGANISM MAY OFFER SHORT-TERM BENEFITS AND ALIGNS WITH CERTAIN ETHICAL VALUES, IT ALSO COMES WITH SIGNIFICANT HEALTH RISKS.

ethical practices and acknowledges animals' role in the ecosystem.

THE PATH TO A MORE HONEST DIET DISCUSSION

The debate between veganism and carnivorism isn't as black-and-white as it's often portrayed. While veganism may offer short-term benefits and align with specific ethical values, it also comes with significant health risks, environmental challenges, and ethical blind spots. The carnivore diet on the other hand, provides essential nutrients in their most bioavailable form and supports sustainable, regenerative agriculture practices that can heal our bodies and the planet.

Rather than framing veganism as the only ethical or environmentally responsible choice, carnivore advocates like Dr. Paul Saladino, Dr. Ken Berry, and Joel Salatin encourage a more nuanced conversation—one that recognizes the complexity of our food systems and the importance of consuming animal products in a way that respects both nature and our health.

By embracing an animal-based diet, we can achieve optimal health, contribute to the restoration of ecosystems, and support ethical farming practices that prioritize animal welfare. The carnivore diet offers an alternative vision of sustainability and health—one that's grounded in biology, regenerative agriculture, and respect for the natural world.

CHAPTER 9
BUDGET FRIENDLY CARNIVORE

Switching to the carnivore diet might sound expensive at first—you might be picturing all those juicy steaks and wondering how you'll afford them. However, the carnivore diet can be quite budget-friendly with the right strategies! You don't need to spend a fortune on fancy cuts of meat to reap the benefits of this diet. In this chapter, we'll explore some tips and tricks to help you enjoy all the protein-packed goodness of the carnivore lifestyle without emptying your wallet.

EMBRACE THE BUDGET-FRIENDLY CUTS

When most people think of the carnivore diet, they imagine high-end cuts like ribeyes and tenderloins. While those are delicious, you don't need them to thrive on this diet. Cheaper cuts like ground beef, chicken thighs, pork shoulder, and chuck roast are all fantastic options. Our family eats these meats most of the time with steak being on the menu once or twice a week. These meats are more affordable and incredibly versatile and flavorful. You can use ground beef in burgers, meatballs, or even casseroles. Chicken thighs are great for roasting or grilling, and pork shoulder is perfect for slowcooking or roasting until tender. These cuts often have a higher fat content - a bonus on the carnivore diet since you want that extra fat for energy.

BUY IN BULK AND FREEZE

One of the best ways to save money on the carnivore diet is to buy in bulk. Look for deals at local grocery stores, butcher shops, or warehouse clubs like Costco. I stock up when I see a good sale, and a small freezer comes in super handy on those days! Meat can be stored in a freezer for months, so buying in larger quantities will save you money in the long run. I portion the meat into meal-sized servings before freezing, so I can grab what I need without having to thaw a huge package all at once.

DON'T FORGET ABOUT ORGAN MEATS

Organ meats, like liver, heart, and kidneys, are nutrient-dense and often much cheaper than muscle meats. These cuts are rich in vitamins and minerals that are essential for your health, making them a great addition to your carnivore diet. If you're new to organ meats, like I was, start by mixing a small amount with ground beef to get used to the taste. You can gradually increase the amount as you become more comfortable with the flavors. This will add variety and nutrition to your diet, plus it will stretch your dollar further.

SHOP AT LOCAL MARKETS AND BUTCHER SHOPS

Local farmers' markets and butcher shops can be great places to find high-quality meats at reasonable prices. These places often have deals on bulk purchases or less popular cuts that grocery stores don't stock. Plus, shopping locally means you're supporting small businesses and potentially getting fresher, more sustainable meat options. Don't be afraid to ask the butcher for recommendations on budget-friendly cuts or any upcoming sales—they're usually more than happy to help!

MAKE USE OF YOUR SLOW COOKER OR INSTANT POT

A slow cooker or Instant Pot can be a game-changer on the carnivore diet. These handy kitchen appliances are wonderful for cooking tougher, cheaper cuts of meat like beef brisket or pork butt, until they're tender and delicious. Plus, they make meal prep a breeze. You can toss in your ingredients in the morning and come home to a hot, ready-to-eat meal. This method is also great for cooking in bulk—make a big batch and have leftovers ready for the rest of the week, saving time and money. My Instant Pot saves the day when I forget to thaw my meat!

SKIP THE FANCY LABELS

While grass-fed, pasture-raised, and organic meats are fantastic if you can afford them, they're not necessary for everyone on the carnivore diet. I am pretty much 50-50 on my budget, but even less "fancy" meat is better than eating processed food or lots of carbs! Conventional meats are still highly nutritious and often come at a fraction of the price. If you're on a tight budget, opting for these more affordable options is perfectly OK. Remember, the goal of the carnivore diet is to focus on animal-based foods, which can be achieved without the premium price tags.

PLAN YOUR MEALS AND REDUCE WASTE

Planning your meals ahead of time can help you save money and reduce food waste. Make a weekly meal plan based on what you have on hand and what's on sale at the store. Use leftovers creatively—yesterday's roast chicken can be today's chicken salad or soup. By making the most of what you buy, you'll get more meals out of the same amount of food, stretching your budget further. You can use the meal plan in Chapter 10 to get started!

CONSIDER CANNED AND FROZEN OPTIONS

Canned and frozen meats, like salmon, sardines, or even chicken, can be a great addition to your carnivore diet. These options are often more affordable and have a longer shelf life, making them perfect for stocking up during sales. Plus, they're just as nutritious as their fresh counterparts and can be used in a variety of dishes, from salads to casseroles.

FINAL THOUGHTS

The carnivore diet doesn't have to be expensive. By choosing budget-friendly cuts, buying in bulk, using organ meats, and planning your meals wisely, you can enjoy all the benefits of this diet without breaking the bank. Remember, be flexible, creative, and resourceful with your choices. With a bit of planning and smart shopping, you'll find that eating a meat-based diet can be affordable and delicious. Happy eating!

CHAPTER

10

30 DAYS OF CARNIVORE MEALS

Here's a 30-day carnivore diet meal plan designed to offer variety, balance, and simplicity while sticking to animal-based foods. The plan includes meals based on beef, pork, poultry, seafood, and eggs, with options for organ meats and higher-fat cuts to ensure you're getting a good balance of nutrients.

WHAT TO EAT: Meat, fish, eggs, and animal fats. Focus on high-quality, nutrient-dense cuts like ribeye, ground beef, chicken thighs, and organ meats. Fatty cuts are encouraged for better satiety and energy.

YOU'LL WANT TO AVOID SAUCES FULL OF SUGAR, SEED OILS, VEGETABLE OILS, SOY, GLUTEN, MSG, OR OTHER PROBLEMATIC INGREDIENTS.

WHAT TO DRINK: Water, bone broth, black coffee, and unsweetened tea are generally accepted. Some people tolerate heavy cream in coffee or tea.

SPICES AND SEASONINGS: However, spices are technically not carnivore since they are not an animal product. Spices and seasonings can be particularly helpful for those transitioning into the carnivore diet, adding variety as you adjust to a more meat-focused way of eating. While many people continue to enjoy using them over time, others find they naturally gravitate toward simpler meals. I tend to stick with just salt on my steaks, and I'm perfectly satisfied with that. Just be aware that plant-based spices can cause a reaction.

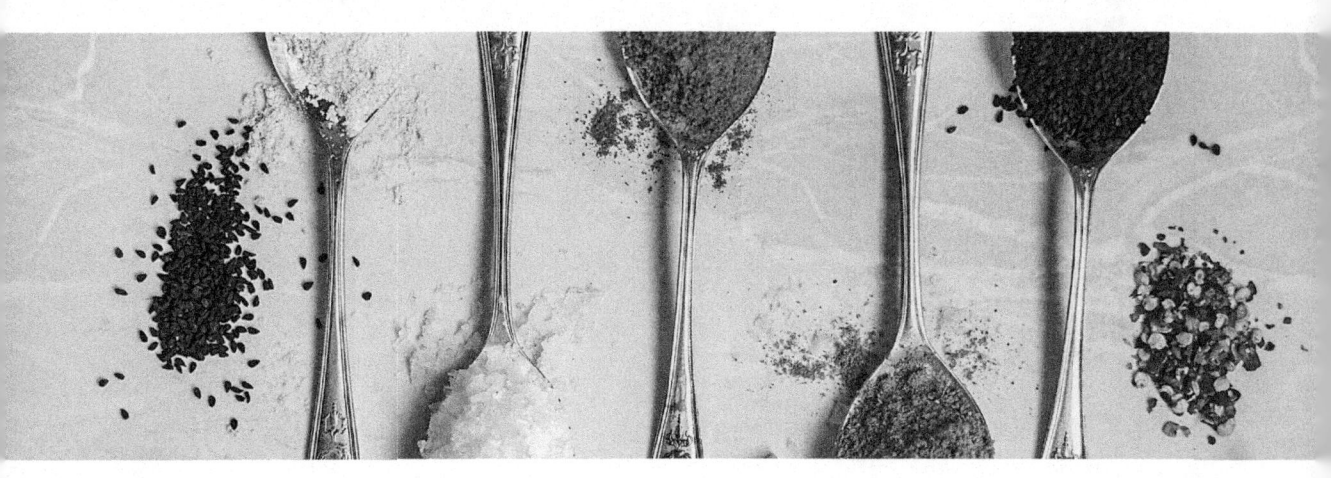

OILS AND FATS : Also, when using sauces, check those ingredients! Avoid sauces full of sugar, seed oils, vegetable oils, soy, gluten, MSG, or other problematic ingredients. If you want to boost flavor, homemade rubs, spice blends, or marinades are good options. Cooking with herbs can also bring out different tastes, but it's essential to pay attention to how your body reacts and remove anything that doesn't agree with you. Remember, the spices I've included in the meals are optional. Salt goes a long way!

TIPS FOR SUCCESS:

STAY HYDRATED: Drink plenty of water, and consider adding electrolytes, especially during the first few weeks.

COOK WITH FAT: Don't be afraid to use butter, tallow, and ghee to add flavor and ensure you're eating enough fat. Avoid seed oils.

EMBRACE VARIETY: While the carnivore diet may seem limited at first, experiment with different cuts of meat, organ meats, and seafood to keep meals exciting.

LISTEN TO YOUR BODY: Eat when you're hungry, and stop when you're full. The carnivore diet is about tuning into your body's natural hunger cues.

WK 1
30 DAYS OF MEAL PLANS

DAY 1

BREAKFAST: 4 scrambled eggs cooked in butter, 4 strips of bacon (season with black pepper, opt.)

LUNCH: Meatloaf, pg. 164

DINNER: Ground beef (80/20) patties with cheddar cheese, seasoned with salt, topped with a fried egg

DAY 2

BREAKFAST: 3 fried eggs seasoned with salt, and served with sausage links (add pepper, fennel and thyme, opt.)

LUNCH: Juicy Baked Chicken Thighs, see pg. 160

DINNER: Pork chops, seasoned with salt, and cooked in lard or bacon grease, topped with butter (add black pepper, opt.)

DAY 3

BREAKFAST: Egg & Bacon Muffins, pg. 143

LUNCH: 2 burger patties seasoned with salt, cooked in butter, topped with bacon (add black pepper, opt.)

DINNER: Crispy Baked Chicken Wings, pg. 166

DAY 4

BREAKFAST: 4 poached eggs seasoned with salt, served with 2 sausage patties (add pepper, and smoked paprika, opt.)

LUNCH: Ribeye steak seasoned with smoked salt, cooked in tallow (add black pepper, opt.)

DINNER: Rotisserie Chicken and Creamy Alfredo Sauce, pg. 169, remove meat from chicken and stir into alfredo sauce

DAY 5

BREAKFAST: 4 boiled eggs with salt, (add black pepper, and a sprinkle of chili flakes, opt.) served with 4 strips of bacon

LUNCH: Bone-in chicken thighs, seasoned with salt, roasted in butter (add oregano, garlic powder, opt.)

DINNER: Lamb chops seasoned with salt, cooked in ghee (add rosemary and a pinch of garlic powder, opt.)

DAY 6

BREAKFAST: Beef liver cooked in butter served with bacon (add garlic and a touch of thyme, opt.)

LUNCH: Fried Chicken Strips, pg. 151

DINNER: Grilled salmon fillet with butter, (add lemon and a pinch of dill, opt.)

DAY 7

BREAKFAST: Crepes, pg. 136

LUNCH: Pork ribs cooked slowly until tender, finished with butter (add garlic, paprika, and cumin, opt.)

DINNER: Filet mignon, seasoned with sea salt, topped with butter mixed with salt (add pepper, garlic powder, and a bit of rosemary, opt.)

WK 2

DAY 8

BREAKFAST: Scrambled eggs with diced ham sauteed in butter (cream cheese diced in egg mixture, opt.)

LUNCH: Ground lamb burgers served with melted cheddar cheese (add cumin, coriander, and a pinch of turmeric, opt.)

DINNER: Bacon Cheeseburger Pie, pg. 167

DAY 9

BREAKFAST: Beef liver, eggs, and bacon, liver seasoned with salt (add black pepper and garlic powder, opt.)

LUNCH: Chaffles, pg. 149

DINNER: Pan-seared ribeye steak seasoned with salt, cooked in beef tallow (add pepper, garlic powder, and paprika, opt.)

DAY 10

BREAKFAST: 4 poached eggs, (add a sprinkle of smoked paprika, opt.) and sausage links (seasoned with fennel and thyme, opt.)

LUNCH: Grilled salmon, with butter, (add lemon zest, garlic powder, dill, opt.).

DINNER: Bacon Wrapped Sea Scallops, pg. 168

DAY 11

BREAKFAST: 3 scrambled eggs with salt, served with beef sausage (add pepper, and a touch of paprika, opt.)

LUNCH: Bone-in pork chops, cooked in ghee (add rosemary, garlic powder, and black pepper, opt.)

DINNER: Pizza, pg. 162

DAY 12

BREAKFAST: Breakfast Casserole, pg. 135

LUNCH: Ground beef bowls seasoned with smoked salt, butter added for richness (add cumin, and garlic, opt.)

DINNER: Bacon Wrapped Liver Bites, pg. 181

DAY 13

BREAKFAST: Pork sausage and fried eggs (seasoned with black pepper and paprika, opt.) cooked in butter

LUNCH: Chicken drumsticks with crispy skin, roasted with salt (add thyme, and garlic, opt.) finished in ghee

DINNER: Ribeye steak with salt, (add pepper, and a garlic-butter drizzle, opt.)

DAY 14

BREAKFAST: Omelet with cheddar, bacon, and salt, cooked in butter (add a sprinkle of smoked paprika, opt.)

LUNCH: Deviled Eggs, pg. 156

DINNER: Grilled pork ribs with salt, (add black pepper, and a smoky dry rub, opt.)

WK 3

DAY 15

BREAKFAST: Scrambled eggs with salt, served with bacon (add smoked paprika, salt, and pepper, opt.)

LUNCH: Ground beef patties seasoned with salt, topped with cheese (add garlic powder, and black pepper, opt.)

DINNER: Meat Loaf, pg. 164

DAY 16

BREAKFAST: Breakfast Bombs, pg.139

LUNCH: Loaded Chicken Salad, pg. 152

DINNER: Pan-seared ribeye steak seasoned with sea salt, topped with butter (add black pepper, garlic powder, and paprika, opt.)

DAY 17

BREAKFAST: Beef liver and 4 scrambled eggs, cooked in butter with salt (add garlic, black pepper, and paprika, opt.)

LUNCH: Quiche, pg. 146

DINNER: Hearty Chili, 165

DAY 18

BREAKFAST: Scotch Eggs, pg. 140

LUNCH: Pork belly pan-fried, served with crispy skin (add garlic, black pepper, and smoked paprika, opt.)

DINNER: Parmesan Crusted Salmon, pg. 161

DAY 19

BREAKFAST: Scrambled eggs served with bacon (add garlic powder and smoked paprika, opt.)

LUNCH: Egg Roll-Ups With Salmon & Cheese Sauce, pg. 155

DINNER: Grilled lamb chops seasoned with salt cooked in ghee (add rosemary, and garlic, opt.)

DAY 20

BREAKFAST: Breakfast Bowl, pg.137

LUNCH: Creamy Chicken Soup, pg. 157

DINNER: Pan-seared steak seasoned with salt, finished with butter (add pepper, garlic powder, and paprika, opt.)

DAY 21

BREAKFAST: 3 fried eggs served with sausage and bacon (add black pepper and smoked paprika, opt.)

LUNCH: Blackened Wild Caught Sockeye Salmon, fried in an iron skillet with butter and salt (add pepper, garlic, smoked paprika, cayenne, or onion powder, opt.)

DINNER: Parmesan Meatballs, pg. 163

WK 4

DAY 22

BREAKFAST: Bacon & Gruyere Sous Vide Egg Bites, pg. 144

LUNCH: Ground beef seasoned with salt, topped with melted cheese (add cumin, garlic, and paprika, opt.)

DINNER: Ribeye steak seasoned with salt topped with butter (add black pepper, garlic, opt.)

DAY 23

BREAKFAST: The Best Omelette, pg. 134

LUNCH: Ground beef patties topped with bacon (seasoned with cumin, garlic powder, and cayenne, opt.)

DINNER: Pork Chops seasoned with salt, cooked in butter (rosemary, garlic, and black pepper, opt.)

DAY 24

BREAKFAST: Beef liver (add garlic, thyme, and black pepper, opt.) served with scrambled eggs

LUNCH: Salmon Patties, pg. 147

DINNER: Lamb chops seasoned with salt (add rosemary, and garlic, opt.) finished with butter

DAY 25

BREAKFAST: Bacon & Brie Frittata, pg. 141

LUNCH: Pork belly roasted (add garlic, thyme, and smoked paprika, opt.) served with crispy skin

DINNER: Pot Roast,

DAY 26

BREAKFAST: Fried eggs served with sausage links (add black pepper and a dash of cayenne, opt.)

LUNCH: Pork Rind Tortillas, pg. 158

DINNER: Ribeye steak with a butter drizzle (seasoned with garlic and black pepper, opt.)

DAY 27

BREAKFAST: Crepes, pg. 136

LUNCH: Bacon Burger & Eggs, pg. 148

DINNER: Chicken drumsticks, roasted, finished with ghee (add garlic, rosemary, and thyme, opt.)

DAY 28

BREAKFAST: Omelet with cheddar and ham, (seasoned with smoked paprika, opt.) cooked in butter

LUNCH: Egg Salad, pg. 153

DINNER: Pork ribs (seasoned with a dry rub of cumin, garlic, smoked paprika, and a dash of cayenne, opt.)

DAY 29

BREAKFAST: Bacon Wrapped Egg Bites, pg. 142

LUNCH: Ground Turkey Muffins, pg. 154

DINNER: Lamb chops seasoned with salt, cooked in ghee and served with a side of pork cracklings (add garlic powder, rosemary, opt.)

DAY 30

BREAKFAST: Biscuits, pg. 138

LUNCH: Ribeye steak seasoned with smoked salt, cooked in butter and topped with a fried egg (add black pepper, and garlic powder, opt.)

DINNER: Pork belly slow-roasted served with crispy pork skin and a drizzle of melted ghee (add garlic, smoked paprika, and a dash of cayenne, opt.)

CHAPTER 11

MOUTHWATERING RECIPES

LET'S START WITH:
BREAK-FAST

THE BEST OMELETTE

PREP TIME: 10 MINUTES | COOK TIME: 20 MINUTES | TOTAL TIME: 30 MINUTES | SERVINGS: 4

INGREDIENTS:

12-16 large eggs
4 slices of bacon
1/2 cup (about 7 oz) 80/20 ground beef
1/4 cup sliced salami (about 3 oz)
3/4 cup Greek yogurt
1 cup shredded mozzarella cheese
2 teaspoons Himalayan pink salt

INSTRUCTIONS:

1. In a large skillet, heat a small amount of oil over medium heat. Add the bacon and cook until crisp. Remove the bacon and set aside. In the same pan, add the ground beef and cook until browned, breaking it up as it cooks.

2. While the meat is cooking, crack the eggs into a large bowl, add the salt, and whisk until well blended.

3. Once the ground beef is cooked, transfer the bacon and beef to a plate. Pour one-fourth of the beaten eggs into the pan, tilting the pan occasionally to let any uncooked egg flow to the edges for even cooking.

4. When the eggs begin to set, add one-fourth of the cooked bacon, beef, salami, Greek yogurt, and mozzarella cheese evenly across one half of the omelet.

5. Allow the omelet to cook for an additional 1–2 minutes until the cheese melts and the eggs are fully set. Carefully fold the omelet in half, then slide it onto a plate. Repeat for the remaining servings. Serve hot and enjoy!

Nutritional Information
(per serving, based on 4 servings):
Calories: 510 kcal, Protein: 40 g, Fat: 38 g, Carbohydrates: 4 g, Net Carbs: 4 g, Cholesterol: 460 mg, Sodium: 950 mg

BREAKFAST CASSEROLE

PREP TIME: 10 MINUTES | COOK TIME: 35-40 MINUTES | TOTAL TIME: 45-50 MINUTES | SERVINGS: 6

This hearty Casserole is packed with protein and flavor, making it a perfect dish for breakfast or meal prep. Containing sausage, eggs, cheese, and a hint of hot sauce, it's a simple and delicious way to start your day.

INGREDIENTS:

12 large eggs
12 oz breakfast sausage
2 cups shredded cheddar cheese
3/4 cup heavy whipping cream
1 tablespoon hot sauce
   (carnivore-friendly)
Salt and pepper to taste

INSTRUCTIONS:

1. Preheat your oven to 350°F (175°C). In a large skillet over medium-high heat, cook the breakfast sausage, using a wooden spoon to break it apart as it cooks. Cook until fully browned but not overcooked.

2. Spread the cooked sausage evenly over the bottom of a 9x13-inch casserole dish.

3. In a large bowl, whisk together the eggs, heavy whipping cream, hot sauce, shredded cheddar cheese, salt, and pepper.

4. Pour the egg mixture evenly over the sausage in the casserole dish.

5. Place the dish in the oven and bake for 35-40 minutes, or until the casserole is fully set and the top is slightly golden. Let the casserole cool for a few minutes before slicing and serving. Enjoy this delicious carnivore-friendly breakfast!

Nutrition Information
(per serving, based on 6 servings):
Calories: 420 kcal, Protein: 26g, Fat: 35g,
Carbohydrates: 2g, Fiber: 0g,
Net Carbs: 2g

CREPES

PREP TIME: 5 MINUTES | COOK TIME: 10 MINUTES | TOTAL TIME: 15 MINUTES | SERVINGS: 2

Made with just a few ingredients, these carnivore pancakes make for a simple and delicious protein-packed breakfast. They're a great alternative for anyone following a carnivore or low-carb diet.

INGREDIENTS:

4 large eggs
4 oz cream cheese, softened
2 tbsp butter or ghee, for cooking
1/4 tsp sea salt
1/4 tsp baking powder
   (optional, for fluffier pancakes)
1 tsp vanilla extract
   (optional, for extra flavor)

INSTRUCTIONS:

1. In a blender or mixing bowl, combine the eggs, softened cream cheese, sea salt, and vanilla extract (if using). Blend or whisk until the mixture is smooth and free of lumps. If you want fluffier pancakes, add the baking powder and blend again.

2. Heat a non-stick skillet or griddle over medium heat. Add a small amount of butter or ghee to grease the pan. Pour small circles of batter (about 2-3 tablespoons) onto the hot pan.

3. Cook for 2-3 minutes, or until bubbles start to form on the surface and the edges are set. Carefully flip the pancakes and cook for another 1-2 minutes until golden brown.

4. Remove the pancakes from the skillet and repeat with the remaining batter. Serve hot with a pat of butter on top, or enjoy as-is for a pure carnivore treat.

Optional Toppings:
Top with more butter or a dollop of whipped cream for added richness. Serve with bacon or sausage on the side for extra protein.

Nutritional Information
(per serving, based on 2 servings):
Calories: 350 kcal, Protein: 14g, Fat: 31g,
Carbohydrates: 3g, Fiber: 0g,
Net Carbs: 3g, Sodium: 400mg

BREAKFAST BOWL

PREP TIME: 10 MINUTES | COOK TIME: 10 MINUTES | TOTAL TIME: 20 MINUTES | SERVINGS: 2

The hearty carnivore breakfast bowl layers scrambled eggs, crispy bacon, and savory ground beef, all topped with melty cheese. It's a delicious, protein-filled way to fuel your morning!

INGREDIENTS:

4 large eggs, scrambled
6 slices cooked bacon, crumbled
1/2 lb ground beef, sautéed
1/2 cup shredded cheddar cheese (or your favorite cheese)
Salt, to taste
Butter or ghee, for cooking

INSTRUCTIONS:

1. In a skillet over medium heat, cook the ground beef until browned and fully cooked. Season with a pinch of salt, then set aside.

2. In the same skillet, melt a little butter or ghee and scramble the eggs. Cook until soft and fluffy, seasoning with salt to taste.

3. In a bowl, layer the scrambled eggs on the bottom. Add the cooked ground beef and crumbled bacon on top. Sprinkle the shredded cheese over the top of the bowl while everything is still hot, allowing the cheese to melt.

4. Enjoy your Carnivore Breakfast Bowl hot and fresh for a satisfying start to your day!

Nutritional Information
(per serving, based on 2 servings):
Calories: 650 kcal, Protein: 45g, Fat: 50g,
Carbohydrates: 2g, Fiber: 0g,
Net Carbs: 2g, Sodium: 1200mg

BISCUITS

PREP TIME: 15 MINUTES | COOK TIME: 12-15 MINUTES | TOTAL TIME: 27-30 MINUTES | SERVINGS: 4

Who knew you could still eat biscuits and be healthy!?! These light and fluffy carnivore Biscuits, are made with crushed pork rinds and whipped egg whites, creating a savory, satisfying bread alternative.

INGREDIENTS:

4 large egg whites
1 cup crushed pork rinds
1 teaspoon baking powder
4 tablespoons cold butter, cubed
1/2 teaspoon salt

INSTRUCTIONS:

1. Preheat your oven to 400°F and line a baking sheet with parchment paper.

2. In a large mixing bowl, beat the egg whites until they form stiff peaks. Set the whipped egg whites aside.

3. In another bowl, mix the crushed pork rinds, baking powder, and salt. Add the cold, cubed butter to the pork rind mixture. Use a fork or pastry cutter to cut the butter into the dry ingredients until it resembles coarse crumbs.

4. Gently fold the whipped egg whites into the pork rind and butter mixture, being careful not to deflate the egg whites too much.

5. Using a spoon, drop dollops of the biscuit dough onto the prepared baking sheet, leaving space between each biscuit.

6. Bake in the preheated oven for 12-15 minutes, or until the biscuits are golden brown and set. Allow the biscuits to cool slightly before serving. Makes 8-10 biscuits depending upon size.

Nutritional Information
(per serving): Calories: 300 kcal,
Protein: 23g, Fat: 23g,
Carbohydrates: 1g, Fiber: 0g,
Net Carbs: 1g, Sodium: 820mg

BREAKFAST BOMBS

PREP TIME: 5 MINUTES | COOK TIME: 0 MINUTES | TOTAL TIME: 15-20 MINUTES-INCLUDES CHILLING | MAKES: 10

Next time you need a protein-packed start to the day, try one of these Breakfast Bombs! Rich and satisfying, they are the ideal grab-and-go option. With creamy, cheesy eggs coated in crispy bacon bits, they're a cinch to make and yummy to eat.

INGREDIENTS:

4 hard-boiled eggs, chopped
6 slices cooked bacon, crumbled
4 oz cream cheese, cubed and softened
Salt and pepper, to taste

INSTRUCTIONS:

1. Chop the hard-boiled eggs into small pieces and place them in a mixing bowl.

2. Add the softened cream cheese cubes to the chopped boiled eggs. Mix everything together until well combined. Season with salt and pepper to taste.

3. Using your hands, form the egg and cream cheese mixture into small bite-sized balls (about 1-2 inches in diameter). Roll each ball in the crumbled bacon bits until fully coated.

4. Place the finished Breakfast Bombs in the fridge for about 10-15 minutes to firm up, or serve them right away.

Nutritional Information
(per serving): Calories: 420 kcal,
Protein: 23g, Fat: 36g, Carbohydrates: 2g,
Fiber: 0g, Net Carbs: 2g, Sodium: 820mg

SCOTCH EGGS

PREP TIME: 15 MINUTES | COOK TIME: 25 MINUTES | TOTAL TIME: 40 MINUTES | SERVINGS: 12 SCOTCH EGGS

Easy Scotch Eggs are a yummy option for breakfast, appetizers, or even a main dish. Scotch eggs can be made with the traditional pork sausage or you can substitute ground beef or even chicken sausage for a tasty variation on the traditional recipe!

INGREDIENTS:

2 pounds ground beef, chicken sausage or pork sausage
2 tablespoons salt
12 large hard-boiled eggs

INSTRUCTIONS:

1. Preheat your oven to 350°F. Line two small rimmed baking sheets with parchment paper.

2. In a large mixing bowl, combine the ground beef, pork sausage or chicken sausage with the salt. Use your hands to mix everything thoroughly.

3. Form the mixture into 12 even-sized meatballs. Flatten each meatball on the baking sheet to form a circle.

4. Place one hard-boiled egg in the center of each circle and wrap the meat around the egg, making sure there are no gaps or holes in the meat.

5. Place the baking sheets in the oven and bake for 10-15 minutes, or until the tops of the meatballs look cooked. Flip the Scotch eggs over and continue baking for another 10 minutes. For a crispier shell, finish the Scotch eggs under the broiler for an additional 5 minutes.

Nutritional Information
(per serving, based on 12 servings):
Calories: 315 kcal, Fat: 24g,
Saturated Fat: 9g, Protein: 25g,
Carbohydrates: 1g, Fiber: 0g,
Net Carbs: 1g, Cholesterol: 465mg,
Sodium: 960mg

BACON & BRIE FRITTATA

PREP TIME: 5 MINUTES | COOK TIME: 12-15 MINUTES | TOTAL TIME: 17-20 MINUTES | SERVES: 4

Combining crispy bacon and creamy Brie makes for a deliciously indulgent breakfast or brunch. It's flavorful and easy to make.

INGREDIENTS:

8 large eggs
1/4 cup heavy cream
6 slices cooked bacon, crumbled
4 oz Brie cheese, sliced
Salt to taste (pepper, opt.)
1 tablespoon butter or ghee

INSTRUCTIONS:

1. In a bowl, whisk together the eggs, heavy cream, and a pinch of salt and pepper until well combined.

2. Heat a large oven-safe skillet over medium heat and add the butter or ghee. Once melted, pour in the egg mixture and spread it evenly in the pan.

3. Add half of the crumbled bacon to the egg mixture. Cook for 7-10 minutes, or until the edges are set and the center is mostly firm.

4. Arrange the Brie slices on top of the frittata and sprinkle the remaining cooked bacon over the top.

5. Place the skillet under the broiler on high for 2-5 minutes, or until the frittata is puffed and the Brie is melted and bubbly. Remove from the oven and let it cool slightly before slicing. Serve hot and enjoy!

Nutritional Information
(per serving, based on 4 servings):
Calories: 400 kcal, Protein: 22g,
Fat: 34g, Carbohydrates: 2g, Fiber: 0g,
Net Carbs: 2g, Sodium: 650mg

BACON-WRAPPED EGG BITES

PREP TIME: 5 MINUTES | COOK TIME: 15-18 MINUTES | TOTAL TIME: 20-30 MINUTES | SERVES: 6

Make these mouthwatering bacon-wrapped egg bites ahead of time for an on-the-go, carnivore-friendly snack or breakfast. Simple and rich in protein, they're quick to prepare and really taste good.

INGREDIENTS:

12 slices of bacon
6 large eggs
1/4 cup heavy cream (optional for added creaminess)
1/2 cup shredded cheddar cheese (optional)
1/2 teaspoon sea salt
1/4 teaspoon black pepper (optional)

INSTRUCTIONS:

1. Preheat your oven to 375°F. Grease a 12-cup muffin tin.

2. Partially cook the bacon slices in a skillet over medium heat for 3-4 minutes, until they are slightly cooked but still pliable. This ensures the bacon will crisp up without burning when baked with the eggs.

3. Line each muffin cup with one bacon slice, forming a ring around the edges.

4. In a bowl, whisk the eggs together with the heavy cream (if using), sea salt, and pepper (optional).

5. Pour egg mixture into each bacon-lined muffin cup, filling them about 3/4 full. If you're using cheese, sprinkle a little shredded cheddar on top of each cup.

6. Place the muffin tin in the preheated oven and bake for 15-18 minutes, or until the eggs are set and the bacon is crispy. Allow the bacon-wrapped egg bites to cool slightly before removing them from the tin. Serve warm.

Optional Add-Ons: Add shredded cheese or cream for extra richness. Incorporate cooked sausage crumbles or diced ham into the egg mixture for added flavor.

Nutritional Information
(per serving, based on 6 servings):
Calories: 210 kcal, Fat: 18g, Protein: 10g,
Carbohydrates: 1g, Fiber: 0g,
Net Carbs: 1g

EGG AND BACON MUFFINS

PREP TIME: 5 MINUTES | COOK TIME: 30-35 MINUTES | TOTAL TIME: 35-40 MINUTES | MAKES: 12

This recipe makes an easy, quick meal on those busy days when you need a healthy breakfast on the go.

INGREDIENTS:

1 1/2 cups egg whites
20 slices Canadian bacon, diced
Salt, to taste (smoked salt recommended for extra flavor)
Pepper, to taste

INSTRUCTIONS:

1. Preheat your oven to 350°F and lightly grease a muffin tin with butter, ghee or bacon grease to prevent sticking.

2. Evenly distribute the diced Canadian bacon into each cup of the muffin tin. Then, pour the egg whites over the bacon, filling each cup just below the rim.

3. Sprinkle salt (add pepper, opt.) over the top of each muffin. For extra flavor, add a little more diced bacon on top.

4. Place the muffin tin in the oven and bake for 30-35 minutes, or until the egg whites are fully cooked. To check for doneness, insert a toothpick into the center of a muffin; it should come out clean.

5. Let the muffins cool in the tin for 10-15 minutes before removing them. Serve warm and enjoy your savory egg and bacon muffins!

Nutrition Information
(per muffin, based on 12 muffins):
Calories: 85 kcal, Fat: 4g, Protein: 11g
Carbohydrates: 0g, Fiber: 0g
Net Carbs: 0g

BACON & GRUYÈRE SOUS VIDE EGG BITES

PREP TIME: 5 MINUTES | COOK TIME: 1 HOUR | TOTAL TIME: 1 HOUR 5 MINUTES | SERVES: 6

A Starbucks copycat, these sous vide egg bites are rich and creamy and packed with the savory flavors of Gruyère cheese and crispy bacon. A great choice for meal prep or a quick protein-loaded snack.

INGREDIENTS:

6 large eggs
1/2 cup heavy cream
1 cup shredded Gruyère cheese
6 slices cooked bacon, crumbled
Sea salt, to taste
Black pepper (optional)

INSTRUCTIONS:

1. In a blender, combine the eggs, heavy cream, shredded Gruyère, salt, and pepper (if using). Blend until smooth and fully combined.

2. Divide the crumbled bacon evenly between small, heat-safe mason jars (4-ounce size works best). Pour the blended egg mixture into the jars, filling each one about 3/4 full.

3. Seal the jars loosely by screwing on the lids just until they catch, but not tightly.

4. Set your sous vide water bath to 172°F. Once the water reaches the desired temperature, carefully place the jars into the water.

5. Cook the egg bites for 1 hour. After 1 hour, remove the jars from the water bath and let them cool slightly before opening. Serve warm, or refrigerate for up to 5 days for an easy grab-and-go snack.

Nutritional Information
(Per Serving, 1 Egg Bite):
Calories: 220 kcal, Protein: 14g, Fat: 18g,
Saturated Fat: 9g, Carbohydrates: 1g,
Fiber: 0g, Sugar: 0g, Cholesterol: 240mg,
Sodium: 350mg, Calcium: 180mg,
Iron: 1mg

TAKE A BREAK FOR :

LUNCH

QUICHE

QUICHE

PREP TIME: 8 MINUTES | COOK TIME: 57 MINUTES | TOTAL TIME: 1 HOUR 5 MINUTES | SERVES: 8

I love quiche for breakfast or a main course and this one hits the spot. With a crunchy pork rind crust and a cheesy filling, it has plenty of flavor going on!

INGREDIENTS:

For the crust:
1 ¼ cups pork rind crumbs
1 ¼ cups freshly grated Parmesan cheese (or hard Gouda cheese)
1 large egg

For the filling:
1/2 cup chicken broth or beef bone broth
1 cup grated Swiss cheese
   (or Muenster cheese)
4 oz cream cheese
1 tablespoon butter, melted
1/2 cup diced ham
4 large eggs, beaten
1/2 teaspoon salt

INSTRUCTIONS:

1. Preheat your oven to 325°F.

2. Prepare the crust: In a mixing bowl, combine the pork rind crumbs and grated cheese. Add the egg and mix until the dough is well combined and stiff. If necessary, add more pork rind crumbs to achieve the right consistency. Press the crust mixture evenly into a 9-inch pie dish, ensuring it is evenly distributed.

3. Bake the crust for 12 minutes, or until it starts to lightly brown.

4. Prepare the filling: In a medium bowl, mix the broth, grated Swiss cheese, melted butter, and cream cheese until well combined. Stir in the diced ham, beaten eggs, and salt.

5. Assemble the quiche: Pour the filling mixture into the pre-baked pie crust. Place the quiche in the oven and bake for 15 minutes at 325°F. Reduce the oven temperature to 300°F and continue baking for an additional 30 minutes, or until a knife inserted 1 inch from the edge comes out clean. If the edges of the crust are browning too quickly, cover them with foil.

6. Let the quiche rest for 10 minutes before slicing into wedges. Serve warm and enjoy!

Nutritional Information
(per serving): Calories: 421 kcal,
Fat: 35g, Saturated Fat: 16g, Protein: 24g,
Carbohydrates: 1g, Fiber: 0g,
Net Carbs: 1g, Cholesterol: 217mg,
Sodium: 890mg

SALMON PATTIES

PREP TIME: 5 MINUTES | COOK TIME: 10 MINUTES | TOTAL TIME: 15 MINUTES | SERVES: 1

Salmon, bacon, and pulled pork come together in this satisfying surf-and-turf dish. These carnivore salmon patties are a delicious blend of rich, savory flavors, ideal for anyone following the carnivore diet.

INGREDIENTS:

3 slices bacon or salted pork belly
2 cans of salmon (6 oz. each)
6 oz. crushed pork rinds
    (use the empty salmon can to measure)
6 oz. pulled pork (Boston Butt works great,
    slow-cooked in a crockpot)
1 tsp salt
2 eggs, whisked
Juice of 1/2 lemon, 1/2 tsp dill (optional)

INSTRUCTIONS:

1. Fry the bacon or pork belly in a pan over medium heat until crispy. Once cooked, crumble the bacon and set it aside. Reserve the bacon grease in the pan for later.

2. In a medium mixing bowl, combine the crumbled bacon, canned salmon, whisked eggs, salt, and optional lemon juice and dill. Stir well.

3. Using the empty 6 oz. Salmon can as a measure, fill it with pulled pork and add the pork to the bowl.

4. Place pork rinds in a ziplock bag and crush them with a mallet or the back of a large spoon. Measure 6 oz. of crushed pork rinds using the salmon can, then add the crushed pork rinds to the bowl.

5. Using your hands, knead all the ingredients together until the mixture is consistent and holds together well.

6. Shape the mixture into 4-6 burger-sized patties.

7. Reheat the pan with the reserved bacon grease over medium-high heat. Once hot, add the patties to the pan. Cook for a few minutes on each side, flipping once browned. Add more butter or bacon grease to the pan as needed during cooking.

8. Enjoy the salmon patties as they are, or with a squeeze of fresh lemon juice. If desired, serve with a low-carb sauce like keto remoulade for an extra kick.

Nutritional Information
(per serving, based on 6 servings):
Calories: 410 kcal, Fat: 31g,
Saturated Fat: 10g, Protein: 31g,
Carbohydrates: 1g, Fiber: 0g,
Net Carbs: 1g, Cholesterol: 160mg,
Sodium: 940mg

BACON, BURGER & EGGS

PREP TIME: 5 MINUTES | COOK TIME: 10 MINUTES | TOTAL TIME: 15 MINUTES | SERVES: 1

I love a fried egg on a burger! Have you ever tried this? I didn't think I would like it but I was wrong! The egg adds so much flavor and, of course, there's the bacon! SO delicious that I don't even miss the bun!

INGREDIENTS:

4 slices of bacon
1/4 lb ground beef patty
1 large egg
Salt to taste (add pepper, opt.)

INSTRUCTIONS:

1. Heat a skillet over medium heat and fry the bacon until crispy. Remove the bacon from the skillet and set it aside, leaving the bacon grease in the pan.

2. In the same skillet with the bacon grease, add the ground beef patty. Season with salt and pepper, and cook for about 3-4 minutes on each side, or until the patty is cooked to your preferred level of doneness. Remove the patty and set it aside.

3. Crack the egg into the skillet, still using the bacon grease, and fry it to your liking (sunny side up, over-easy, etc.). Season with a pinch of salt and pepper.

4. Place the cooked burger patty on a plate, top with the crispy bacon slices, and then place the fried egg on top to complete the stack.

Nutritional Information
(per serving): Calories: 460 kcal, Protein: 30g, Fat: 36g, Carbohydrates: 1g, Fiber: 0g, Net Carbs: 1g, Sodium: 900mg

BASIC CHAFFLES

PREP TIME: 5 MINUTES | COOK TIME: 5 MINUTES | TOTAL TIME: 10 MINUTES | SERVES: 2

I love to make chaffles and we make them a LOT at my place! You can use a wide variety of ingredients and the result is a warm, crunchy snack, stand-alone meal or bread replacement. Be sure to try the variations too!

INGREDIENTS:

1 cup shredded cheese (cheddar, mozzarella, or Parmesan work best)
2 large eggs

Optional Add-Ons:
1/2 tsp garlic powder or onion powder for extra flavor (optional)
A pinch of salt (if your cheese is not already salty enough)
2 slices of cooked bacon, chopped (for extra texture and flavor)

INSTRUCTIONS:

1. Preheat your waffle maker according to the manufacturer's instructions.

2. In a mixing bowl, whisk together the eggs. Add the shredded cheese and mix until well combined. If using, stir in the optional garlic powder, onion powder, or chopped bacon.

3. Lightly grease the waffle maker using butter, ghee or tallow if necessary. Pour about half of the mixture into the preheated waffle maker, spreading it evenly. Close the waffle maker and cook for 3-5 minutes, or until the chaffle is golden brown and crispy on the outside.

4. Remove the chaffle from the waffle maker and set aside. Repeat with the remaining mixture. Serve hot, and enjoy on its own or use as a sandwich or burger bun replacement.

TRY THESE TASTY CHAFFLE VARIATIONS!

BACON & CHEDDAR

INGREDIENTS:

2 large eggs
1 cup shredded cheddar cheese
2 slices cooked, crumbled bacon
1/4 teaspoon black pepper (optional)

HERBED PARMESAN

INGREDIENTS:

2 large eggs
1 cup shredded Parmesan cheese
1/4 teaspoon dried rosemary or thyme (optional)
Pinch of garlic powder (optional)

CREAM CHEESE

INGREDIENTS:

2 large eggs
4 tablespoons softened cream cheese
1/2 cup shredded mozzarella cheese
Pinch of salt

PEPPERONI PIZZA

INGREDIENTS:

2 large eggs
1 cup shredded mozzarella cheese
3-4 slices pepperoni, chopped
1/4 teaspoon oregano (optional)

SAUSAGE & GOUDA

INGREDIENTS:

2 large eggs
1 cup shredded Gouda cheese
2 tablespoons cooked, crumbled sausage
Pinch of salt and pepper

Nutritional Information
(per serving, based on 2 servings)

Basic Chaffle
Calories: 340 kcal, Protein: 26 g, Fat: 26 g, Carbohydrates: 2 g, Net Carbs: 2 g, Cholesterol: 370 mg, Sodium: 650 mg

Bacon & Cheddar Chaffle
Calories: 440 kcal, Protein: 31 g, Fat: 34 g, Carbohydrates: 2 g, Net Carbs: 2 g, Cholesterol: 375 mg, Sodium: ~950 mg

Herbed Parmesan Chaffle
360 kcal, Protein: 30 g, Fat: 24 g, Carbohydrates: 2 g, Net Carbs: 2 g, Cholesterol: 430 mg, Sodium: 880 mg

Cream Cheese Chaffle
290 kcal, Protein: 20 g, Fat: 22 g, Carbohydrates: 2 g, Net Carbs: 2 g, Cholesterol: 425 mg, Sodium: 560 mg

Pepperoni Pizza Chaffle
Calories: 420 kcal, Protein: 33 g, Fat: 32 g, Carbohydrates: 2 g, Net Carbs: 2 g, Cholesterol: 430 mg, Sodium: 940 mg

Sausage & Gouda Chaffle
Calories: 480 kcal, Protein: 35 g, Fat: 38 g, Carbohydrates: 2 g, Net Carbs: 2 g, Cholesterol: 430 mg, Sodium: 900 mg

FRIED CHICKEN STRIPS

PREP TIME: 20 MINUTES | COOK TIME: 50 MINUTES | TOTAL TIME: 1 HOUR 20 MINUTES | SERVES: 4

These Fried Chicken Strips are the best and I fry them up in my air fryer almost every week!! The strips are tender, crispy, and a great sub for ChickFila! Enjoy the classic taste of fried chicken without the carbs and unhealthy oils.

INGREDIENTS:

1 lb chicken thighs or tenders
6 oz pork cracklings (or pork rinds)
2 eggs
Sea salt (to taste)

INSTRUCTIONS:

1. Prepare the breading: Take your pork cracklings and blend them in a blender until they reach the consistency of a fine, oily powder. (Note: Pork rinds will also work, but pork cracklings create a thicker, crunchier coating.) Transfer the pork crackling powder into a medium-sized bowl.

2. Cut the chicken strips: Cut the chicken thighs into strips, about 4 inches long and 1/2-1 inch wide, or adjust the size to your preference.

3. Coat the chicken: In a separate small bowl, beat the eggs. Dip each chicken strip into the pork crackling powder, then into the beaten egg, and finally back into the pork crackling powder. Ensure each strip is fully coated with a thick, even layer of breading.

4. Cooking options:

Oven method: Preheat your oven to 400°F. Place the coated chicken strips on a parchment paper-lined baking sheet. Salt the strips generously. Bake for 20 minutes, then flip the strips and bake for an additional 20-25 minutes, until the coating is hard and crunchy.

Air fryer method: Set your air fryer to 400°F. Place the chicken strips in the air fryer basket and cook for 20 minutes. Flip them over and cook for an additional 20 minutes until crispy.

5. Serve hot with your favorite dipping sauce.

Nutritional Information
Calories: 556.5, Protein: 55.5g,
Fat: 35.5g, Carbohydrates: 0.25g

LOADED CHICKEN SALAD

PREP TIME: 10 MINUTES | SERVINGS: 2

You've never had a chicken salad this scrumptious! Rich and flavorful, this carnivore-friendly dish is packed with protein and healthy fats. It's quick to make and a great choice for a delicious meal.

INGREDIENTS:

1 can (12.5 oz) canned chicken, drained
2 tablespoons mayonnaise
   (see homemade version below)
2 tablespoons sour cream
Black pepper, to taste
Garlic powder, to taste
3 slices bacon, cooked and chopped
1.5 oz cheddar cheese, shredded
Parsley or dill for garnishing (optional)

INSTRUCTIONS:

1. Drain the canned chicken and add it to a large mixing bowl.

2. Add the mayonnaise and sour cream to the bowl with the chicken. If desired, season with black pepper and garlic powder to taste.

3. Add the chopped bacon and shredded cheddar cheese. Mix all the ingredients thoroughly until well combined.

4. Garnish with parsley or dill if desired, and serve with carnivore bread or enjoy on its own.

Nutrition Information
(per serving): Calories: 380 kcal
Protein: 35g   Fat: 28g
Carbohydrates: 1g   Fiber: 0g
Net Carbs: 1g

EGG SALAD

PREP TIME: 5 MINUTES | COOK TIME: 12 MINUTES | TOTAL TIME: 17 MINUTES | SERVES: 3

I love a good egg salad and this recipe fits the bill. It's a simple, tasty, and protein-based dish that's great for breakfast, lunch, or even a snack. Made with eggs, sour cream, and mustard, it's a quick meal option when you need food fast.

INGREDIENTS:

6 large eggs
1 tablespoon sour cream
3/4 teaspoon mustard
Black pepper, to taste (optional)
Salt, to taste
Garlic powder or other seasonings (optional

INSTRUCTIONS:

1. Boil the eggs: Bring a pot of water to a boil. Add the eggs, cover the pot, and cook for 7 minutes.

2. Cool the eggs: While the eggs are cooking, prepare a bowl of ice water. Once the eggs are done, transfer them to the ice water for 5 minutes to cool. Peel the eggs once they are cooled.

3. Mash the eggs: Place the peeled eggs in a serving bowl. Add the sour cream, mustard, salt, and pepper. Mash everything together until smooth.

4. Season and serve: Adjust the seasoning to taste, adding garlic powder or other seasonings or a parsley garnish if desired.

Nutritional Information
(per serving, based on 2 servings):
Calories: 150 kcal, Fat: 12g,
Saturated Fat: 4g, Protein: 9g,
Carbohydrates: 1g, Fiber: 0g,
Net Carbs: 1g, Cholesterol: 375mg,
Sodium: 320mg

GROUND TURKEY MUFFINS

PREP TIME: 10 MINUTES | COOK TIME: 20-25 MINUTES | TOTAL TIME: 30-35 MINUTES | SERVINGS: 12

Make these savory ground turkey muffins ahead of time for an easy lunch on the go. This high-protein breakfast or snack is loaded with flavor from the cheese and butter, while the eggs keep them fluffy and satisfying.

INGREDIENTS:

1 lb ground turkey
8 large eggs
1 cup shredded cheddar cheese
1/2 cup grated Parmesan cheese
1/4 cup heavy cream
1/4 cup melted butter
2 teaspoons salt

INSTRUCTIONS:

1. Preheat your oven to 350°F and grease a 12-cup muffin tin.

2. In a skillet over medium heat, cook the ground turkey until fully browned. Season with 1 teaspoon of salt while cooking. Remove from heat and set aside.

3. In a large mixing bowl, whisk together the eggs, heavy cream, melted butter, and the remaining 1 teaspoon of salt.

4. Stir in the cooked ground turkey, shredded cheddar cheese, and grated Parmesan cheese into the egg mixture until evenly distributed.

5. Spoon the mixture into the prepared muffin tin, filling each cup about 3/4 full.

6. Place in the preheated oven and bake for 20-25 minutes, or until the muffins are set and golden brown on top.

7. Allow the muffins to cool slightly before removing them from the tin. Serve warm, or store in an airtight container in the refrigerator for up to 3 days.

Nutritional Information
(per serving, based on 6 servings):
Calories: 420 kcal, Fat: 31g,
Saturated Fat: 14g, Protein: 36g,
Carbohydrates: 2g, Fiber: 0g,
Net Carbs: 2g, Cholesterol: 365mg,
Sodium: 1080mg

EGG ROLL-UP WITH SALMON & CHEESE SAUCE

PREP TIME: 10 MINUTES | COOK TIME: 10-12 MINUTES | TOTAL TIME: 20-22 MINUTES | SERVINGS: 3-4

I could eat this Egg Roll with Salmon and Cheese Sauce every day- it's that good! The smoked salmon pairs beautifully with the creamy cheddar cheese sauce, making a luscious treat!

INGREDIENTS:

For the egg rolls:
6 large eggs
2 tablespoons heavy cream
Sea salt, to taste
4 oz smoked salmon, sliced

For the cheese sauce:
1/2 cup heavy cream
1/2 cup shredded cheddar cheese
2 tablespoons butter
Sea salt, to taste

INSTRUCTIONS:

Prepare the egg roll-ups:
1. In a medium bowl, whisk together the eggs, 2 tablespoons of heavy cream, and a pinch of sea salt until smooth and well combined.

2. Heat a non-stick skillet over medium heat and lightly grease it with butter, ghee, tallow or bacon grease. Pour about 1/4 cup of the egg mixture into the pan and swirl to create a thin, crepe-like layer.

Cook for 2-3 minutes, or until the egg is set and the edges begin to pull away from the pan. Carefully flip and cook the other side for about 1 minute.

3. Transfer the cooked egg crepe to a plate. Repeat the process with the remaining egg mixture to make 3-4 egg rolls.

4. Place a few slices of smoked salmon on each egg crepe. Gently roll up the egg crepe like a wrap or burrito and set aside.

Prepare the cheese sauce:

1. In a small saucepan over medium heat, add 1/2 cup of heavy cream and 2 tablespoons of butter. Heat until the butter melts and the mixture starts to simmer.

2. Gradually whisk in the shredded cheddar cheese, stirring constantly until the cheese is fully melted and the sauce is smooth and creamy. Add sea salt to taste.

3. Place the egg rolls with smoked salmon on a plate. Generously drizzle the warm cheddar cheese sauce over the egg rolls. Serve as a hearty breakfast or satisfying lunch!

Nutritional Information
(per serving, based on 2 servings):
500k cal, 42g Fat, 23g Saturated Fat, 28g Protein, 3g Carbohydrates, 0g Fiber, 3g Net Carbs, 465mg Cholesterol, 850mg Sodium

DEVILED EGGS

PREP TIME: 10 MINUTES | COOK TIME: 20-25 MINUTES | TOTAL TIME: 30-35 MINUTES | SERVINGS: 12

An excellent snack or appetizer, these simple and satisfying carnivore deviled eggs are made with just a few ingredients for a creamy, flavorful treat.

INGREDIENTS:

6 hard-boiled eggs
1/4 cup creamy mayonnaise (pg 179)
Salt, to taste (pepper and paprika, opt.)

INSTRUCTIONS:

1. Peel the hard-boiled eggs and slice them in half lengthwise. Remove the yolks and place them in a bowl.

2. Mash the yolks with the homemade carnivore mayonnaise and a pinch of salt until smooth and creamy.

3. Spoon or pipe the yolk mixture back into the egg white halves. Arrange the deviled eggs on a plate and serve immediately, or refrigerate until ready to enjoy.

....

Nutritional Information
(per serving, based on 3 servings):
Calories: 190 kcal, Protein: 9g, Fat: 17g, Carbohydrates: 1g, Fiber: 0g, Net Carbs: 1g, Sodium: 230mg

CREAMY CHICKEN SOUP

PREP TIME: 10 MINUTES | COOK TIME: 20 MINUTES | TOTAL TIME: 30 MINUTES | SERVINGS: 4

The next time you need a comforting meal, make this Creamy Chicken Soup. This rich and satisfying dish is made with simple ingredients like chicken, cream cheese, and an egg. It's a homey, easy to prepare meal.

INGREDIENTS:

12 oz cooked chicken breast, shredded
8 oz cream cheese
3 cups chicken broth
1 whole egg
1 tablespoon garlic, minced
1 1/2 teaspoons black pepper (optional)
1 1/2 teaspoons salt (smoked salt recommended)

INSTRUCTIONS:

1. In a slow cooker, combine the cooked chicken, cream cheese, chicken broth, garlic, black pepper, and salt. Cook on low for 2.5 to 3 hours until the ingredients are well heated and combined.

2. Before serving, carefully ladle about 2 cups of the soup into a blender. Turn the blender on, starting at a low speed and gradually increasing to high. While blending, slowly add the egg and continue blending until smooth.

3. Pour the blended soup back into the slow cooker and stir well until fully combined with the rest of the soup.

4. Ladle the creamy carnivore chicken soup into bowls and enjoy a rich, flavorful meal!

Nutritional Information (per serving): 397 kcal, Fat: 42g, Saturated Fat: 22g, Protein: 44g, Carbohydrates: 5g, Fiber: 0g, Net Carbs: 5g, Cholesterol: 250mg, Sodium: 1650mg.

PORK RIND TORTILLAS

PREP TIME: 10 MINUTES | COOK TIME: 15 MINUTES | TOTAL TIME: 25 MINUTES | SERVINGS: 4

Made with simple ingredients like pork rinds, eggs, and ghee, these Pork Rind Tortillas are low-carb, gluten-free, and a tasty alternative to traditional tortillas. Try them with tacos or other dishes.

INGREDIENTS:

5 oz pork rinds (pre-ground or grind your own)
6 large eggs
1 tablespoon grass-fed ghee or butter (plus extra for cooking)
2 cups water
1 teaspoon sea salt

INSTRUCTIONS:

1. First, prepare the pork rind batter: If you're using whole pork rinds, grind them into a fine powder using a blender or food processor. In the blender, add the pork rind powder, eggs, 1 tablespoon of ghee or butter, water, and sea salt. Blend until the mixture becomes smooth and has a liquid consistency similar to a thin milkshake. If the batter thickens as it sits, simply add a little more water to maintain the proper consistency.

2. Next, cook the tortillas: Heat an 8-inch non-stick pan over low-medium heat. Add a small amount of ghee or butter (about 1 teaspoon) to grease the pan. Pour just under 1/4 cup of the batter into the pan, starting from the center and spiraling out to fill the pan evenly. The batter should be thin enough to cover the pan without curling up around the edges. If the pan is too hot and the batter sizzles, remove it from the heat and let it cool slightly before pouring the next batch. Cook the tortilla for about 7 minutes on one side, then flip it and cook for an additional 3 minutes on the other side. Adjust cook times based on your stovetop heat.

3. Repeat: After each tortilla, remove the pan from the heat and re-grease with more ghee or butter. Repeat the process with the remaining batter, adding water to thin it if necessary. Continue cooking until all the batter is used.

4. Use these tortillas for tacos, wraps, or as a base for your favorite fillings. Enjoy your delicious carnivore-friendly meal!

Tips: Ensure the pan stays well-lubricated with ghee or butter between tortillas to prevent burning.

Nutritional Information
(per serving, based on 4 servings:
340 kcal, Fat: 25g, Saturated Fat: 8g,
Protein: 25g, Carbohydrates: 2g,
Fiber: 0g, Net Carbs: 2g,
Cholesterol: 300mg, Sodium: 750mg.

IT'S ALMOST TIME FOR:

DINNER

JUICY BAKED CHICKEN THIGHS

JUICY BAKED CHICKEN THIGHS

PREP TIME: 10 MINUTES | COOK TIME: 30 MINUTES | TOTAL TIME: 40 MINUTES | SERVINGS: 4

This might be the best chicken recipe ever! SO flavorful and juicy that both Chris and I are amazed every time we make it, and we make it a LOT!

INGREDIENTS:

2 tablespoons ghee or butter
2 teaspoons smoked salt

Optional Seasonings:
2 teaspoons garlic powder
2 teaspoons onion powder
1 teaspoon ground paprika
1 teaspoon Italian seasoning
1 teaspoon dried parsley
1/2 teaspoon black pepper

2 pounds chicken thighs (6-8 pieces), patted dry
1 tablespoon butter, diced

INSTRUCTIONS:

1. Preheat your oven to 400°F. Place a cast iron skillet in the oven while it heats up to get the pan nice and hot.

2. In a large bowl, mix the ghee and seasonings to form a paste.

3. Add the chicken thighs to the bowl with the seasoning paste. Toss the chicken in batches if necessary, making sure to coat each thigh evenly and rub the seasoning into the skin.

4. Carefully remove the hot pan from the oven and place the seasoned chicken thighs on it. Dot the chicken with the diced butter for added flavor and moisture. Bake for 20 minutes.

5. After 20 minutes, carefully remove the chicken from the oven and baste the thighs with the pan juices. Return the chicken to the oven and bake for an additional 10 minutes. Baste again, then bake for another 5-15 minutes until the chicken reaches an internal temperature of 165°F. Let the chicken rest for a few minutes before serving.

Nutritional Information
(per serving): 347 kcal, Fat: 28g, Protein: 21g, Carbohydrates: 2g, Fiber: 1g, Net Carbs: 1g.

PARMESAN CRUSTED SALMON

PREP TIME: 10 MINUTES | COOK TIME: 17-20 MINUTES | TOTAL TIME: 27-30 MINUTES | SERVINGS: 4

This Parmesan crusted salmon recipe is a scrumptious, crunchy, and satisfying dish just right for those on a carnivore diet. I make this recipe a lot because I love the crispy crust made from the pork rinds and parmesan cheese. If you struggle with cooking salmon, try this version!

INGREDIENTS:

1 lb. salmon fillet
2 tablespoons butter, melted (divided)
3/4 cup crushed pork rinds
1/4 cup Parmesan cheese, grated
Salt, to taste
Black pepper, to taste (optional)
1 teaspoon lemon zest (optional)
1/4 teaspoon dried thyme
   (omit for strict carnivore diet)

INSTRUCTIONS:

1. Preheat your oven to 370°F.

2. Season the salmon fillets with salt, black pepper, and any optional seasonings like lemon zest or thyme. Place the salmon, skin side down, in a greased baking dish. Brush the top of the salmon with half of the melted butter.

3. In a bowl, combine the crushed pork rinds, Parmesan cheese, and the remaining melted butter.

4. Press the pork rind-Parmesan mixture firmly onto the top of each salmon fillet, ensuring an even layer.

5. Place the baking dish in the oven and bake for 17-20 minutes, depending on the thickness of the fillets. The salmon should flake easily with a fork when done.

6. Remove the salmon from the oven and let it cool for about 10 minutes. Serve and enjoy!

Nutritional Information
(per serving, based on 4 servings):
380 kcal, Fat: 28g, Protein: 29g,
Carbohydrates: 1g, Fiber: 0g,
Net Carbs: 1g.

PIZZA

PREP TIME: 10 MINUTES | COOK TIME: 15-23 MINUTES | TOTAL TIME: 25-33 MINUTES | SERVINGS: 4

Pizza is one of my favorite foods! (Isn't it everyones'?) This healthy version let's you still enjoy an Italian classic.

INGREDIENTS:

Crust:
1 lb. ground chicken for the crust
1/2 cup shredded mozzarella cheese, divided in half
1 teaspoon Italian seasoning (optional)
1/2 cup shredded cheddar cheese
1/4 cup Parmesan cheese
Salt to taste
Pepper to taste (optional)
1/2 cup cooked bacon or sausage
1/2 cup shredded or sliced cheese or choice for extra toppings (optional)
Italian, garlic, and oregano seasonings to taste (optional)

INSTRUCTIONS:

1. Preheat your oven to 400°F.

2. In a mixing bowl, combine the ground chicken, 1/2 c mozzarella, the Italian seasoning, and a pinch of salt and pepper. Mix well until the ingredients are thoroughly combined.

3. Spread the chicken mixture onto a parchment-lined baking sheet or pizza pan. Use your hands or a spatula to flatten it into a thin, round shape, about 1/4 inch thick, resembling a pizza crust. Make sure it's evenly spread to ensure even cooking.

4. Bake the ground chicken crust for 20 minutes. Remove from the oven and carefully soak up any excess juice with a paper towel.

5. For optional toppings:
Sprinkle 1/2 c of shredded mozzarella cheese evenly over the pre-baked meat crust. Add cheddar or your favorite cheese blend, bacon or sausage, and seasonings, if using.

6. Return the pizza to the oven and bake for another 5-8 minutes, or until the cheese is fully melted and bubbly.

7. For a more decadent finish, sprinkle Parmesan cheese on top before serving. Slice and serve your carnivore pizza hot. Enjoy!

Nutritional Information
(Per serving): 450 kcal, 37.5 g protein, 32.5 g fat, 1 g carbs, 0 g fiber, 0.5 g sugars, 250 mg calcium, 600 mg sodium, 125 mg cholesterol.

PARMESAN MEATBALLS

PREP TIME: 10 MINUTES | COOK TIME: 15-20 MINUTES | TOTAL TIME: 25-30 MINUTES | SERVINGS: 4

These cheesy meatballs are a great, savory treat! Made with simple ingredients, they're delicious, filling, and ideal for a quick snack, easy lunch, or even a main meal.

INGREDIENTS:

1 lb. ground beef (80/20) or ground pork
1 egg
1/4 cup grated Parmesan cheese
2 tbsp heavy cream
   (optional, for extra richness)
Salt to taste (pepper, optional)
1/2 tsp garlic powder (optional)
1/2 tsp onion powder (optional)

INSTRUCTIONS:

1. Preheat your oven to 375°F. In a large mixing bowl, combine the ground beef, egg, grated Parmesan cheese, heavy cream (if using), salt to taste (pepper, garlic powder, and onion powder, opt). Mix the ingredients until well combined, but avoid overmixing to keep the meatballs tender.

3. Roll the meat mixture into small balls, about 1-2 inches in diameter, and place them on a parchment-lined baking sheet.

4. Bake in the preheated oven for 15-20 minutes, or until the meatballs are cooked through and lightly browned on the outside.

5. Enjoy the meatballs as-is, or serve them with a side of melted butter, or drizzle with beef or pork broth for added flavor.

Nutritional Information
(per serving, based on 4 servings):
350 kcal, Fat: 25g, Protein: 28g,
Carbohydrates: 1g, Fiber: 0g,
Net Carbs: 1g.

MEATLOAF

PREP TIME: 10 MINUTES | COOK TIME: 45-60 MINUTES | TOTAL TIME: 55-70 MINUTES | SERVINGS: 6

This carnivore meatloaf recipe is a fan favorite because it's rich, satisfying, and versatile. You can customize it with different spices or toppings while staying true to the carnivore diet. The addition of bacon and Parmesan cheese elevates the flavor, making it a hearty meal.

INGREDIENTS:

2 lbs ground beef (80/20)
2 eggs
1/2 cup grated Parmesan cheese
1/4 cup pork rinds, crushed
1/4 cup heavy cream
Salt to taste
Pepper to taste (optional)
1 tsp garlic powder (optional)
1 tsp onion powder (optional)
4 slices of bacon (optional, for topping)

INSTRUCTIONS:

1. Preheat your oven to 375°F.

2. In a large mixing bowl, combine the ground beef, eggs, Parmesan cheese, crushed pork rinds, heavy cream, salt, pepper, garlic powder, and onion powder. Mix everything until well combined, but be careful not to overmix to keep the meatloaf tender.

3. Form the meat mixture into a loaf shape and place it in a loaf pan, or shape it by hand and place it on a parchment-lined baking sheet.

4. If using bacon, lay the slices over the top of the meatloaf, slightly overlapping one another for extra flavor and moisture.

5. Bake in the preheated oven for 45-60 minutes, or until the meatloaf is cooked through (internal temperature of 160°F. Let the meatloaf rest for about 10 minutes before slicing and serving. Enjoy!

Nutritional Information
(per serving, based on 6 servings):
450 kcal, Fat: 35g, Protein: 30g,
Carbohydrates: 2g, Fiber: 0g,
Net Carbs: 2g.

HEARTY CHILI

PREP TIME: 10 MINUTES | COOK TIME: 15-20 MINUTES | TOTAL TIME: 25-30 MINUTES | SERVINGS: 6

This chili is easy to throw together, making it a great choice for a quick meal for those busy workdays or hectic weekends.

INGREDIENTS:

3 pounds ground meat
 (beef, pork, or a mix)
1 tablespoon smoked salt
1/2 - 1 cup beef broth or water
 (adjust to preferred consistency)

Optional Seasonings:
2 tablespoons cumin
2 tablespoons chili powder
1 tablespoon smoked paprika
1 teaspoon black pepper
1 teaspoon cayenne pepper
 (optional for extra heat)
Grated cheese (optional, for topping)

INSTRUCTIONS:

1. In a large skillet or pot, brown the ground meat over medium heat, breaking it up as it cooks.

2. Once the meat is browned, add the cumin, chili powder, smoked paprika, black pepper, cayenne pepper (if using), and salt. Stir well to coat the meat with the spices.

3. Pour in the beef broth or water, adjusting the amount to reach your desired chili consistency. Mix everything thoroughly and let it simmer for about 5-10 minutes to allow the flavors to meld.

4. Once done, serve the chili hot, and if desired, top with grated cheese. For an extra twist, you can also add a fried egg on top.

Nutritional Information
(per serving, based on 8 servings):
320 kcal, Fat: 22g, Protein: 28g,
Carbohydrates: 2g, Fiber: 1g,
Net Carbs: 1g, Sodium: 950mg.

CRISPY BAKED CHICKEN WINGS

PREP TIME: 10 MINUTES | COOK TIME: 40-42 MINUTES | TOTAL TIME: 50-52 MINUTES | SERVINGS: 4

These chicken wings are full of flavor and make for a simple, satisfying meal. Whether baked or air-fried, they come out crispy every time! I personally love the air-fried version- they are ready in no time!

INGREDIENTS:

2 lbs. chicken wingettes
2 tbsp oil
  (ghee, tallow, butter, or bacon grease)
1-2 tbsp baking powder
1 tsp smoked salt

Optional Seasonings:
1 tsp black pepper
1 tsp paprika
1 tsp garlic powder
1 tsp onion powder
1 tsp chili powder

INSTRUCTIONS:

1. Preheat your oven to 425°F.

2. In a large bowl, toss the chicken wingettes with avocado oil and baking powder until evenly coated. Add the salt. Add pepper, paprika, garlic powder, onion powder, and chili powder, if using mixing well to ensure the wings are fully seasoned.

3. Arrange the wings on a wire rack placed on a baking sheet. Bake for 40 minutes, flipping the wings halfway through the cooking time to ensure even crisping.

4. For extra crispy wings, broil for the last 1-2 minutes.

Air Fryer Method: Preheat your air fryer to 400°F. Air fry the wings for 25-30 minutes, shaking halfway through for even cooking.

Enjoy your crispy, flavorful chicken wings!

Nutritional Information
(per serving, based on 4 servings):
420 kcal, Fat: 30g, Protein: 36g,
Carbohydrates: 2g, Fiber: 1g,
Net Carbs: 1g, Sodium: 900mg.

BACON CHEESEBURGER PIE

PREP TIME: 10 MINUTES | COOK TIME: 25-30 MINUTES | TOTAL TIME: 35-40 MINUTES | SERVINGS: 4

I love cheeseburgers and this bacon pie version is delicious! Easy to make, it's loaded with ground beef, bacon, cheddar cheese, and rich cream, making a mouthwatering meal that combines all the flavors of a classic cheeseburger.

INGREDIENTS:

1.5 pounds ground beef
6 slices bacon, chopped
3 large eggs
7 oz cheddar cheese, shredded, divided
5 fl oz heavy cream/double cream
Butter (for greasing)
1/2 teaspoon salt
Black pepper to taste (optional)

INSTRUCTIONS:

1. Preheat your oven to 400°F. Grease a frying pan with butter.

2. Chop three slices of bacon and add them to the pan with the ground beef, salt, and pepper. Cook until lightly browned. Transfer the cooked beef and bacon mixture to a greased baking dish.

3. Crack the eggs into a bowl and whisk them. Pour the eggs into the baking dish over the meat. Add the heavy cream and half of the shredded cheddar cheese. Mix everything well.

4. Top the pie with the remaining cheddar cheese and the chopped pieces of the remaining three slices of bacon.

5. Bake in the preheated oven for 25-30 minutes, or until the cheese is melted and bubbly, and the pie is golden brown. Let it cool for 10 minutes before slicing and serving.

Nutritional Information
(per serving, based on 6 servings):
550 kcal, Fat: 45g, Protein: 35g,
Carbohydrates: 2g, Fiber: 0g,
Net Carbs: 2g.

BACON-WRAPPED SEA SCALLOPS

PREP TIME: 10 MINUTES | COOK TIME: 11 MINUTES | TOTAL TIME: 21 MINUTES | SERVINGS: 4

INGREDIENTS:

16 large sea scallops, cleaned and pat dry with paper towels
8 slices thick-cut bacon
Melted oil, ghee, butter or tallow
Freshly ground black pepper, to taste (optional)
16 toothpicks (for securing the bacon)

INSTRUCTIONS:

1. Set your air fryer to 400°F and preheat for 3 minutes.

2. Lay the bacon slices in the air fryer basket and cook for 3 minutes, flipping halfway through, until they begin to crisp but remain flexible. Set the bacon on paper towels to cool slightly.

3. Remove the side muscles from the scallops, if present, and thoroughly pat them dry with paper towels to remove excess moisture.

4. Wrap each scallop with a half slice of bacon and secure with a toothpick.

5. Brush the scallops with melted oil and sprinkle with freshly ground black pepper if desired. Place the scallops in a single layer in the air fryer basket, ensuring they are not touching. Cook for 8 minutes, turning halfway through, until the scallops are tender and the bacon is crispy.

6. Remove the toothpicks before serving, and enjoy while hot.

Nutritional Information
(per serving, based on 4 servings):
180 kcal, Fat: 8g, Protein: 25g, Carbohydrates: 0g, Fiber: 0g, Net Carbs: 0g, Sodium: 500mg.

CREAMY ALFREDO SAUCE

PREP TIME: 10 MINUTES | COOK TIME: 5 MINUTES | TOTAL TIME: 15 MINUTES | SERVINGS: 4

This rich and creamy sauce is so flavorful you won't believe it's good for you! But it is!

INGREDIENTS:

1/2 cup grated Parmesan cheese
1 1/2 cups heavy cream
1 tablespoon butter
Salt to taste (try pepper or smoked pepper for extra flavor, opt.)

INSTRUCTIONS:

1. In a medium saucepan, melt the butter over medium-low heat.

2. Add the heavy cream and bring it to a simmer, allowing it to cook for about 5 minutes.

3. Reduce the heat to low and slowly whisk in the Parmesan cheese until the sauce is smooth and creamy.

4. Season with salt and pepper to taste.

5. Remove from heat, let it cool slightly, and serve over your favorite carnivore dishes!

Nutritional Information
(per serving, based on 4 servings):
320 kcal, Fat: 31g, Protein: 5g,
Carbohydrates: 2g, Fiber: 0g,
Net Carbs: 2g, Sodium: 450mg.

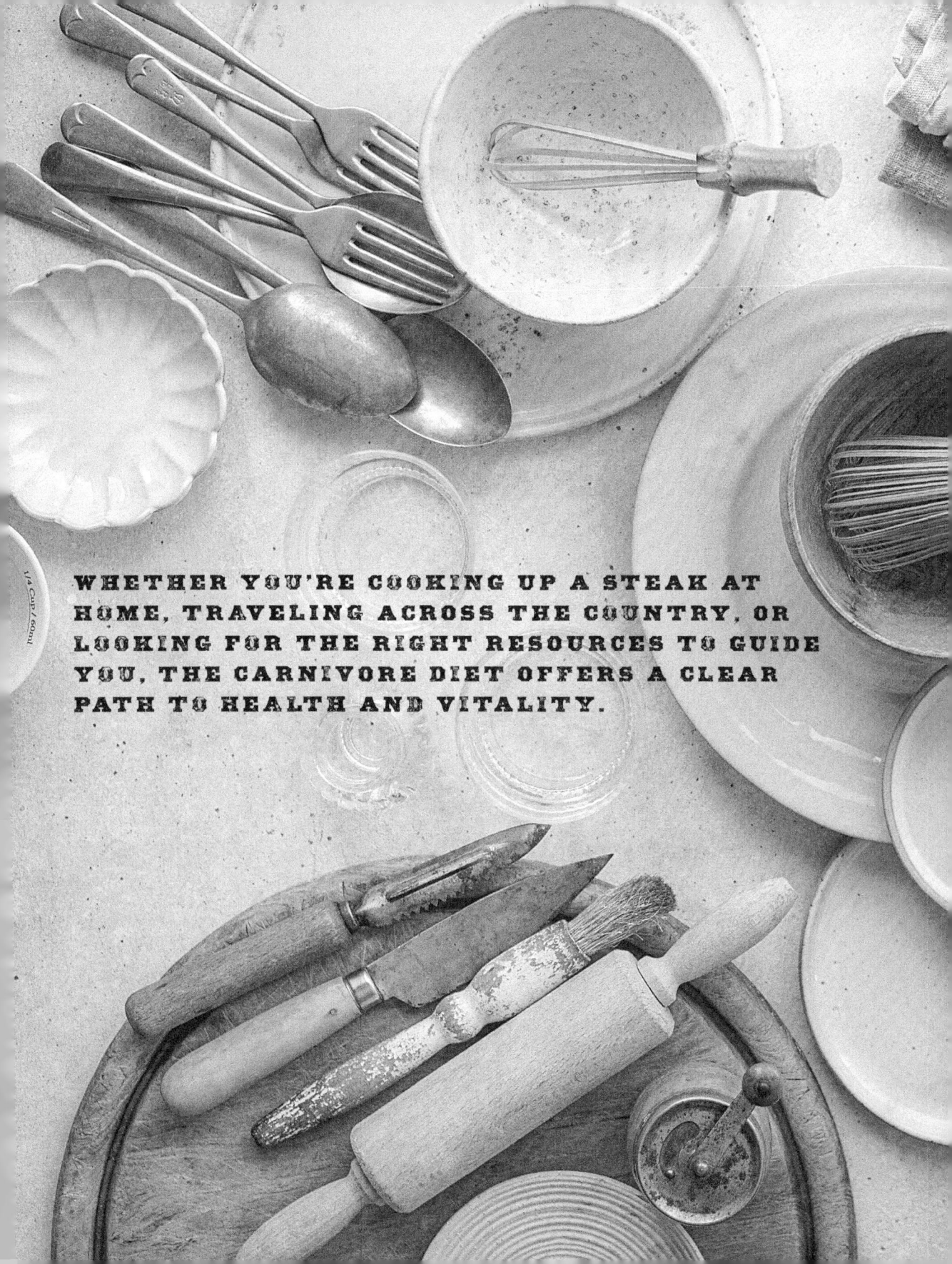

WHETHER YOU'RE COOKING UP A STEAK AT HOME, TRAVELING ACROSS THE COUNTRY, OR LOOKING FOR THE RIGHT RESOURCES TO GUIDE YOU, THE CARNIVORE DIET OFFERS A CLEAR PATH TO HEALTH AND VITALITY.

THERE IS ALWAYS ROOM FOR:
SNACKS & EXTRAS

FRIED MOZZARELLA STICKS

PREP TIME: 10 MINUTES | COOK TIME: 10 MINUTES | TOTAL TIME: 20 MINUTES | SERVINGS: 20 STICKS

You gotta try these fried mozzarella sticks! Coated with pork rinds and fried to golden perfection, I think you'll love these cheesy bites as much as I do!

INGREDIENTS:

5 oz pork rinds, finely crushed
2 large eggs
10 string mozzarella cheese sticks, halved
1/2 teaspoon Italian seasoning (optional)
Tallow for frying (or your preferred frying fat)

INSTRUCTIONS:

1. Heat tallow or your chosen frying fat in a deep pan or skillet to around 370°F.

2. Cut each string mozzarella stick in half to create 20 shorter pieces.

3. In a food processor, blend the pork rinds until finely crushed. Mix in the Italian seasoning, if using. In a separate bowl, whisk the eggs thoroughly.

4. Dip each mozzarella stick into the whisked eggs, coating it completely. Then roll it in the pork rind mixture, ensuring it's evenly covered. For a thicker coating, dip the cheese stick back into the egg mixture and then into the pork rinds again for a second layer.

5. Fry a few cheese sticks at a time in the hot oil for about 1 minute, or until golden and crispy. If you notice the cheese starting to leak, remove them immediately. Repeat with the remaining cheese sticks.

6. Serve hot and enjoy your crispy, cheesy carnivore mozzarella sticks!

Nutritional Information
(per serving): 200 kcal, Fat: 15g, Protein: 15g, Carbohydrates: 1g, Fiber: 0g, Net Carbs: 1g.

CREAMY POPSICLES

PREP TIME: 10 MINUTES | COOK TIME: 10 MINUTES | TOTAL TIME: 20 MINUTES | SERVINGS: 4

These creamy popsicles are the ideal indulgent treat for those on a carnivore or low-carb diet. Made with rich mascarpone cheese, heavy whipping cream, and a hint of cocoa, these popsicles are a chocolaty treat.

INGREDIENTS:

5.5 oz whole milk
5.5 oz mascarpone cheese
5.5 oz heavy whipping cream
1 teaspoon vanilla powder (optional)
3/4 teaspoon unsweetened cocoa powder (optional)

INSTRUCTIONS:

1. In a small saucepan over low heat, combine the milk, cocoa powder, heavy whipping cream, and vanilla powder. Stir continuously to avoid scorching and ensure everything is well mixed. Heat until just warmed, then remove from the heat.

2. Let the mixture cool for about 20 minutes.

3. In a blender, add the mascarpone cheese. Once the milk mixture has cooled, pour it into the blender with the mascarpone. Blend until the mixture is smooth and well combined.

4. Pour the blended mixture into popsicle molds. Freeze overnight, or for at least 6 hours, until fully frozen.

5. Once frozen, remove the popsicles from the molds and enjoy your delicious, creamy carnivore treat!

Nutritional Information
(per serving, based on 4 servings):
150 kcal, Fat: 13g, Protein: 3g,
Carbohydrates: 3g, Fiber: 0g,
Net Carbs: 3g.

ICE CREAM

PREP TIME: 15 MINUTES | COOK TIME: 10 MINUTES | TOTAL TIME: 25 MINUTES + FREEZING TIME | SERVINGS: 2

Ice cream has always been my weakness so having a healthy version was so exciting! This carnivore ice cream is a luscious, creamy treat that's made with just 4 simple ingredients, is easy to prepare, and is a great substitute!

INGREDIENTS:

2 large eggs
11.8 oz heavy whipping cream
1 tablespoon vanilla extract (optional)
2 tablespoons monk fruit or xylitol (optional for sweetness)

INSTRUCTIONS:

1. Separate the egg yolks from the whites. Whisk the egg yolks until they are fluffy and smooth, then set them aside.

2. In a saucepan, combine the heavy whipping cream, sweetener, and vanilla extract. Bring the mixture to a boil, then reduce to a simmer. Stir continuously until the cream thickens.

3. Lower the heat and gradually whisk the whipped egg yolks into the cream mixture. Continue stirring until the mixture thickens again.

4. Remove the saucepan from the heat and let the mixture cool down for at least 30 minutes.

5. While the mixture cools, beat the egg whites until fluffy. Once the cream mixture has cooled, gently fold the egg whites into it.

6. Pour the ice cream mixture into a jar or container with a tight-fitting lid. Shake the contents, then place the jar in the freezer. Stir the mixture every 1-2 hours until it reaches the desired frozen consistency.

7. Once fully frozen, scoop out the ice cream and enjoy this creamy carnivore treat!

Nutritional Information
(per serving, based on 2 servings):
250 kcal, Fat: 25g, Protein: 4g,
Carbohydrates: 2g, Fiber: 0g,
Net Carbs: 2g.

CREAM CHEESE BITES

PREP TIME: 10 MINUTES | COOK TIME: 8-10 MINUTES | TOTAL TIME: 18-20 MINUTES | SERVINGS: 6-8 BITES

You're going to love these crispy cream cheese bites! They're a fantastic snack or appetizer, coated in crushed pork rinds and air-fried to a golden crisp. Creamy on the inside and crunchy on the outside, they're sure to be a hit!

INGREDIENTS:

2 large eggs, slightly beaten
8 oz cream cheese (cold brick, sliced)
2 oz pork rinds, crushed

INSTRUCTIONS:

1. Slice the cold cream cheese into 6-8 equal pieces. Roll each piece into a ball.

2. In a small bowl, whisk the eggs with a fork. Set aside.

3. Place the pork rinds in a plastic bag and crush them using a rolling pin or food processor. Transfer the crushed pork rinds to a separate medium bowl.

4. Dip each cream cheese ball into the beaten eggs, ensuring it's fully coated. Then, roll the ball in the crushed pork rinds, pressing gently to adhere. Shake off any excess coating.

5. Preheat your air fryer to 400°F. Place the coated cream cheese balls in the air fryer basket, ensuring they're not touching. Air fry for 8-10 minutes, or until crispy and golden brown.

6. Allow the cream cheese bites to cool slightly before serving. Enjoy them while they're warm and crispy!

Nutritional Information
(per serving): 347 kcal, Fat: 28g, Protein: 21g, Carbohydrates: 2g, Fiber: 1g, Net Carbs: 1g.

CREAMY DREAMY CUSTARD

PREP TIME: 10 MINUTES | COOK TIME: 30 MINUTES | TOTAL TIME: 40 MINUTES | SERVINGS: 4

These little custards have been a game changer in our household. Sometimes I make them several days in a row, they're THAT good! We make custard for a dessert but it could also be eaten at breakfast time. (Sometimes I add a few drops of stevia or monk fruit powder if I'm wanting a sweet dessert.) When I remember that a dish of custard is still in my fridge, is it wrong to be so excited? Try it and see what you think!

INGREDIENTS:

3 whole eggs
2 cups heavy cream
1 tablespoon vanilla extract (optional)

INSTRUCTIONS:

1. Preheat your oven to 350°F.

2. In a large bowl, whisk together the eggs, heavy cream, and vanilla extract until the mixture is completely smooth.

3. Divide the mixture evenly into 4 ramekins (2-3 inches in diameter) and place them in an 8×8-inch baking dish.

4. In a small saucepan, bring 2-3 cups of water to a boil. Carefully pour the boiling water into the baking dish to create a water bath, filling until the water reaches about 1 inch high.

5. Bake the custard for 30 minutes. Check for doneness—if needed, continue baking for an additional 10 minutes. The top should be golden brown and firm, while the inside should remain slightly wiggly.

6. Remove from the oven and let the custard cool for about 10 minutes. Serve warm or refrigerate until chilled to let it firm up further.

Nutritional Information
(per serving, based on 4 servings):
375 kcal, Fat: 38g, Saturated Fat: 23g,
Protein: 6g, Carbohydrates: 4g,
Fiber: 0g, Net Carbs: 4g,
Cholesterol: 285mg, Sodium: 50mg.

CARNIVORE WHITE BREAD

PREP: 15 MINUTES | COOK: 45 MIN. | REST TIME: 45 MIN. | TOTAL TIME: 1 HR 45 MIN. | SERVINGS: 12 SLICES

When you are craving a sandwich, this recipe will save the day! Skip the wheat allergies and still enjoy a slice of bread, carnivore style!

INGREDIENTS:

4 large eggs (separated)
7 heaping Tbsp egg white powder (separated 4 and 3)
¾ cup heavy whipping cream
1 ½ Tbsp unflavored gelatin
2 tsp white vinegar (optional)
1 tsp baking soda
1-2 tsp instant bread yeast (optional)

INSTRUCTIONS:

1. Preheat oven to 325° F

2. In a large bowl add 4 egg whites and 3 heaping Tbsp of egg white powder. (Make sure bowl is clean or egg whites will not whip)

3. Whip whites to soft peaks and add baking soda. Mix again until stiff peaks, scraping sides as necessary.

4. In a separate mixing bowl, add cream and whip to a soft creamy texture.

5. Add gelatin to whipped cream, sprinkling evenly over the surface. Mix immediately to avoid clumps, beating until the cream is thick.

6. Add egg yolks, vinegar, 4 Tbsp of egg white powder and yeast to the whipped cream. Mix on low just until all clumps of powder are mixed in. Avoid over mixing.

7. Gently fold in the egg white fluff into whipped cream bowl, until all white streaks are gone and mixture is an even color. Avoid over mixing.

8. Grease bread pan with animal fat of your choice. Add mixture into pan and smooth out top.

9. Bake on middle oven rack for 45 minutes.

10. After the bread has finished baking, turn off oven and crack oven door slightly. Let bread and oven cool together for 45 minutes.

11. Remove rested loaf from oven and allow to cool to room temperature.

12. Turn loaf upside down for easy slicing.

13. Store bread slices in an airtight container for up to 1 week in the refrigerator or 3 months in the freezer. Thaw in Refrigerator 2-3 days before using.

....

Nutritional Information
(per slice, based on 12 slices): 110 kcal, Protein: 10g, Fat: 7g, Carbohydrates: 1g, Fiber: 0g, Net Carbs: 1g, Cholesterol: 90mg, Sodium: 170mg.

CREAMY MAYONNAISE

PREP TIME: 10 MINUTES | TOTAL TIME: 10 MINUTES | SERVING: 1 CUP

Add richness to any meal with this creamy mayonnaise. Made from animal-based ingredients, it pairs perfectly with meat dishes and adds a burst of flavor to any meal.

INGREDIENTS:

1 large egg yolk
1 teaspoon apple cider vinegar or lemon juice
1 cup beef tallow, bacon fat, or melted ghee (cooled to room temperature)
1/2 teaspoon sea salt

INSTRUCTIONS:

1. In a medium mixing bowl, whisk together the egg yolk and apple cider vinegar (or lemon juice) until well combined.

2. Slowly start to drizzle in the melted fat (beef tallow, bacon fat, or ghee) while continuously whisking. It's important to add the fat gradually to help the mayonnaise emulsify properly.

3. Continue whisking and drizzling the fat until the mayonnaise thickens to your desired consistency. This process can also be done using an immersion blender for ease.

4. Once the mayonnaise is thick and creamy, add the sea salt and stir to combine.

5. Transfer the mayonnaise to an airtight container and refrigerate. It will keep for up to a week in the fridge.

Nutrition Information
(per tablespoon, based on 16 servings):
Calories: 100 kcal   Fat: 11g
Saturated Fat: 4g   Protein: 0.3g
Carbohydrates: 0g   Fiber: 0g
Net Carbs: 0g   Cholesterol: 25mg
Sodium: 100mg

BONE MARROW

PREP TIME: 5 MINUTES | COOK TIME: 20 MINUTES | TOTAL TIME: 25 MINUTES | SERVINGS: 2

Bone marrow is a nutrient-rich delicacy that's incredibly simple to prepare. It's rich in healthy fats and essential nutrients like collagen, making it a great addition to a carnivore diet.

INGREDIENTS:

4 large beef marrow bones
   (preferably grass-fed)
Sea salt to taste
Freshly ground black pepper (optional)
1-2 tablespoons of butter or tallow
   (optional, for extra richness)

INSTRUCTIONS:

1. Preheat your oven to 450°F.

2. Place the marrow bones, cut side up, on a baking sheet lined with parchment paper. Lightly sprinkle the marrow with sea salt and, if desired, black pepper.

3. Roast the marrow bones in the preheated oven for 15-20 minutes, or until the marrow is bubbly and soft, but not completely melted. The marrow should easily pull away from the bone with a spoon.

4. Remove the bones from the oven, and allow them to cool slightly. Spoon the marrow out of the bones and serve immediately, spreading it over a steak, or enjoy it on its own.

Optional Step: For added richness, melt butter or tallow over the top before serving.

Nutritional Information
(per serving, based on 4 servings):
Calories: 290 kcal, Protein: 6g,
Fat: 28g, Carbohydrates: 0g, Fiber: 0g,
Net Carbs: 0g, Sodium: 200mg

BACON-WRAPPED LIVER BITES

PREP TIME: 10 MINUTES | COOK TIME: 10 MINUTES | TOTAL TIME: 20 MINUTES | SERVINGS: 12 BITES

These bacon-wrapped liver bites are a flavorful and nutrient-packed carnivore snack or appetizer. With crispy bacon on the outside and tender liver on the inside, they're a great way to add liver to your menu. Enjoy this savory dish hot out of the oven!

INGREDIENTS:

1 lb liver, sliced into 1-inch thick, 3-inch-long pieces
12 slices bacon
Sea salt, to taste
Toothpicks

INSTRUCTIONS:

1. Preheat your oven to 400°F (200°C).

2. Slice the liver into pieces that are about 1 inch thick and 3 inches long.

3. Wrap each piece of liver with a slice of bacon, securing it with a toothpick.

4. Sprinkle a bit of sea salt on top of each bacon-wrapped liver bite.

5. Place the wrapped liver bites on a baking sheet and bake for about 10-12 minutes, or until the bacon is crispy and golden brown.

6. Remove from the oven and enjoy your bacon-wrapped liver bites hot!

Nutritional Information
(per serving, 2-3 bites): 190 kcal,
Fat: 8.4g, Protein: 22g,
Carbohydrates: 1g, Fiber: 0g,
Sodium: 600mg, Cholesterol: 180mg.

CINNAMON CRUNCH TREAT

PREP TIME: 5 MINUTES | SERVINGS: 2

This treat will surprise you! It's so simple but so good!

INGREDIENTS:

1.5 oz Pork Rinds
1 tablespoon Butter melted
1 teaspoon Cinnamon

(Using cinnamon is not Carnivore but if used sparingly it can be tolerated by some.)

INSTRUCTIONS

1. Combine the melted butter and cinnamon in a resealable plastic bag. Mix well.

2. Add the pork rinds to the bag. Seal the bag and shake gently to coat all the pork rinds evenly.

3. Transfer the coated pork rinds to a serving bowl. Serve and enjoy this carnivore-friendly snack!

Nutritional Information (per serving): 235 kcal, Fat: 20g, Protein: 13g, Carbohydrates: 1g, Fiber: 1g, Net Carbs: 0g

PREP TIME: 10 MINUTES | COOK TIME: 24 HOURS | TOTAL TIME: 24 HOURS 10 MINUTES | SERVINGS: 8

This rich, nutrient-dense Bone Broth provides essential minerals and gelatin for gut health. It's simple to make and can be enjoyed on its own or used in various recipes.

INGREDIENTS:

4 oz mixed animal bones (beef, lamb, pork, or chicken)
2 teaspoons salt (optional, use pink Himalayan salt for added minerals)
4 liters of water (enough to cover the bones, with a 1:2 broth ratio)
2 tablespoons apple cider vinegar or lemon (helps extract minerals from the bones, opt.))

INSTRUCTIONS:

1. Set your oven to 230°F.

2. Arrange the bones in a single layer on a deep roasting tray. Sprinkle with salt and roast for about 30 minutes, turning halfway through. The bones are ready when they turn a rich, caramelized brown. (This step is optional but adds extra flavor.)

3. Transfer the roasted bones and any juices into a large pot. Add water and apple cider vinegar if desired. Bring the mixture to a boil, then reduce the heat to low, allowing the broth to simmer gently.

4. For the first two hours, skim the foam from the top every 15 minutes to keep the broth clear. (If you prefer, you can skip skimming as the foam is protein and fat.)

5. Allow the broth to simmer for at least 18-24 hours, adding extra water as needed to ensure the bones stay covered.

6. After the broth is done, let it cool slightly. Strain it through a fine-mesh strainer or cheesecloth into glass jars. Store in the fridge for up to five days or freeze for up to six months.

RECIPE TIPS:

Cooking Times: Adjust cooking times based on the type of bones. Fish broth takes around 2 hours, chicken broth 12 hours, and beef, lamb, or pork broth 24 hours.

Marrow Bones: For added calcium, simmer the broth longer to extract the marrow.

Slow Cooker: You can also use a slow cooker for ease, especially for longer cooking times.

Odor Control: Keep the kitchen fan on during cooking to minimize the smell.

Foam: Skimming the foam results in a clearer broth, but leaving it will give a darker, richer broth packed with protein and fat.

Uses: Bone broth can be used as a base in other dishes, like braised meats, scrambled eggs, or pate.

NUTRITIOUS BONE BROTH

Nutritional Information (per serving): 20 kcal, Protein: 5g, Fat: 1g, Carbohydrates: 0g, Sodium: 500mg, Calcium: 10mg, Iron: 0.5mg.

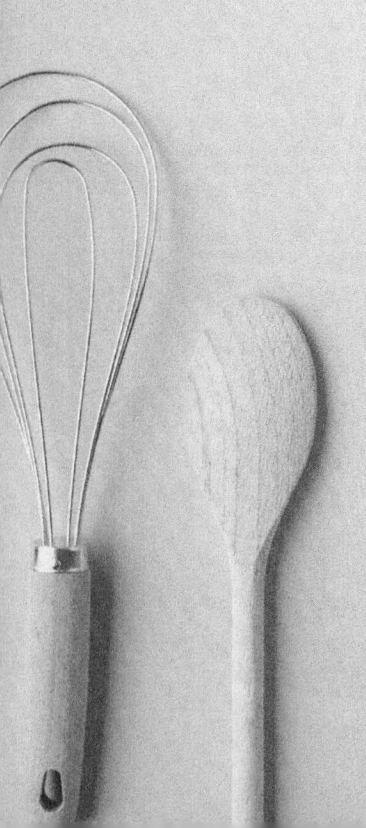

CHAPTER 12
RESOURCES

Getting started with the carnivore diet can feel overwhelming, but luckily, there are plenty of resources to help guide you through it. Whether you're looking for meal inspiration, scientific studies, or community support, there are books, podcasts, websites, and online forums dedicated to the carnivore lifestyle.

One of the best places to begin is Dr. Shawn Baker's *The Carnivore Diet*, which provides a comprehensive look at the science behind the diet, common questions, and how to approach the lifestyle. *Carnivore Cure* by Judy Cho is another great resource that dives deeper into the biochemical mechanisms of how the carnivore diet affects your health.

Websites like MeatRx (now known as Revero) offer meal plans, testimonials, and coaching to help people thrive on an all-meat diet. These communities allow you to connect with others on the same journey, share experiences, and gain advice. The forums also offer insights on how to tackle specific challenges, such as transitioning into carnivore or dealing with cravings.

For podcasts, The Fundamental Health Podcast by Dr. Paul Saladino and The Carnivore Cast are excellent listens that offer interviews with experts, success stories, and advice on how to optimize your carnivore diet. Listening to these regularly can provide motivation and education, especially when you're starting out or looking for answers to specific questions.

Here's a list of

50

community support resources, books, podcasts, websites, and online forums dedicated to the carnivore lifestyle, providing a wide range of information and inspiration for those on or curious about the diet.

COMMUNITY SUPPORT & FORUMS

Meatrx.com – Online community and coaching for the carnivore diet

Zeroing in On Health (ZIOH) – Facebook group for carnivore support

World Carnivore Tribe – Large Facebook group dedicated to the carnivore diet

Carnivore Diet Support Group – Facebook group with resources and discussion

r/carnivore (Reddit) – Reddit forum with discussions, success stories, and Q&A

Carnivore Diet Success Stories (MeatRx.com) – Personal success stories shared by people thriving on the diet

Strict Carnivore – Facebook group focusing on strict carnivore without cheats or exceptions

Carnivore Hard Core – Facebook group for strict carnivores with no plant-based foods

The Carnivore Diet 30-Day Challenge – Facebook group dedicated to helping new carnivores get started

The Ketogenic Forum – While primarily keto, many discussions cover carnivore topics

BOOKS

The Carnivore Diet
by Dr. Shawn Baker – A comprehensive guide by a leading advocate of the carnivore diet

The Carnivore Code
by Dr. Paul Saladino – A deep dive into the carnivore diet's benefits and science

The Carnivore Cookbook
by Jessica Haggard – A cookbook packed with carnivore-friendly recipes

The Fat of the Land by Vilhjalmur Stefansson – The account of an Arctic explorer who lived on a carnivorous diet

Keto Animal Foods by Judy Cho – A guide to incorporating animal-based nutrition into your diet

Sacred Cow
by Diana Rodgers and Robb Wolf – Discusses the nutritional, environmental, and ethical reasons for eating meat

Carnivore Cure
by Judy Cho – A comprehensive guide to healing the body through a meat-based diet

The Ketogenic Bible
by Dr. Jacob Wilson and Ryan Lowery – Though focused on keto, it includes a section on the carnivore diet

Lies My Doctor Told Me
by Dr. Ken Berry – Breaks down common nutritional myths and advocates for low-carb and carnivore eating

The Big Fat Surprise
by Nina Teicholz – A defense of meat and fat as healthy, debunking myths surrounding saturated fat

PODCASTS

The Human Performance Outliers Podcast – Hosted by Dr. Shawn Baker, this podcast discusses carnivore topics, health, and fitness.

Fundamental Health Podcast – Dr. Paul Saladino interviews experts on topics surrounding carnivorous eating and health.

MeatRx Podcast – Dr. Shawn Baker's official podcast featuring carnivore success stories.

Peak Human Podcast – Brian Sanders interviews experts on carnivore, keto, and ancestral health.

Boundless Body Radio – Explores topics of health, fitness, and the carnivore diet with guests.

Carnivore Cast – Hosted by Scott Myslinski, it features interviews with health experts, athletes, and others following the carnivore lifestyle.

The Keto Savage Podcast – Robert Sikes interviews guests on keto, carnivore, and fitness.

Nutrition with Judy Podcast – Judy Cho covers topics related to the carnivore diet and healing through nutrition.

Carnivore and Beyond Podcast – Focuses on low-carb and carnivorous lifestyles, featuring various guest interviews.

WEBSITES

MeatRx.com – A hub for carnivore support, including coaching, resources, and testimonials.

CarnivoreMD.com – Dr. Paul Saladino's site with blogs, resources, and research on the carnivore diet.

Shawn-Baker.com – Official website of Dr. Shawn Baker, featuring his work, podcast, and carnivore resources.

NutritionwithJudy.com – Judy Cho's website with blogs, resources, and carnivore meal plans.

KevinStock.io – Dr. Kevin Stock's website on health, fitness, and the carnivore diet.

KetogenicGirl.com – Features carnivore recipes and resources.

PrimalEdgeHealth.com – Offers carnivore and ketogenic recipes, blogs, and guides.

TheCarnivoreCast.com – Companion site for the Carnivore Cast podcast with resources and interviews.

Ketogenic.com – Features articles and resources, including carnivore diet guides.

YOUTUBE CHANNELS

Shawn Baker MD – Dr. Shawn Baker's YouTube channel covering carnivore topics, health tips, and interviews.

Carnivore MD – Dr. Paul Saladino's YouTube channel diving deep into carnivore diet science and health.

KenDBerryMD – Dr. Ken Berry shares insights on low-carb, carnivore, and keto diets.

Carnivore Yogi – A channel sharing experiences, tips, and insights on the carnivore diet.

MeatRx TV – Offers a wide range of success stories, carnivore coaching, and interviews with experts.

Steak and Butter Gal – Bella shares her vegan-to-carnivore story and offers tips and advice about the carnivore lifestyle.

What I've Learned – Health and fitness YouTube channel with videos on the benefits of the carnivore diet.

Primal Edge Health – Tristan covers topics on ancestral health, carnivore, and keto diets.

Frank Tufano – A carnivore-focused channel discussing nutrition, health, and sustainable meat-eating.

Bart Kay – Nutrition science watchdog Bart Kay dives into the science behind low-carb, carnivore, and ancestral diets.

WRAPPING IT UP

The carnivore diet is simple, yet it's powerful in its ability to transform health and well-being. By focusing on nutrient-dense animal foods and eliminating the noise of processed and plant-based products, you give your body what it needs to function at its best. Though it may seem unconventional at first, many find that this way of eating is more sustainable and easier than they ever imagined.

Yes, there are challenges—especially when it comes to affordability, cooking, and traveling—but with a few practical strategies, these can easily be overcome.

Whether you're cooking up a steak at home, traveling across the country, or looking for the right resources to guide you, the carnivore diet offers a clear path to health and vitality.

Ultimately, the carnivore diet is about taking control of your health by simplifying your diet down to its most essential components. As you embrace this lifestyle, you'll learn to listen to your body, focus on real food, and experience the benefits that come from nourishing yourself with what you're biologically designed to eat.

REFERENCES

CHAPTER 1

Baker, Shawn. The Carnivore Diet. Victory Belt Publishing, 2019.

Taubes, Gary. Good Calories, Bad Calories: Fats, Carbs, and the Controversial Science of Diet and Health. Alfred A. Knopf, 2007.

Hite, Gretchen, et al. "Systematic Review of the Effect of Dietary Saturated Fat on Heart Disease." Journal of the American College of Nutrition, vol. 29, no. 6, 2010, pp. 601-608.

Ludwig, David S., et al. "The Science of Low-Carbohydrate Diets." Annual Review of Nutrition, vol. 38, 2018, pp. 269-288.

Saladino, Paul. The Carnivore Code. Houghton Mifflin Harcourt, 2020.

Siri-Tarino, P. W., Sun, Q., Hu, F. B., & Krauss, R. M. (2010). Meta-analysis of prospective cohort studies evaluating the association of saturated fat with cardiovascular disease. American Journal of Clinical Nutrition, 91(3), 535-546. https://doi.org/10.3945/ajcn.2009.27725

Chowdhury, R., Warnakula, S., Kunutsor, S., Crowe, F., Ward, H. A., Johnson, L., Franco, O. H. (2014). Association of dietary, circulating, and supplement fatty acids with coronary risk: a systematic review and meta-analysis. Annals of Internal Medicine, 160(6), 398-406. https://doi.org/10.7326/M13-1788

Mozaffarian, D., Micha, R., & Wallace, S. (2010). Effects on coronary heart disease of increasing polyunsaturated fat in place of saturated fat: a systematic review and meta-analysis of randomized controlled trials. PLoS Medicine, 7(3), e1000252. https://doi.org/10.1371/journal.pmed.1000252

CHAPTER 2

Baker, Shawn. The Carnivore Diet. Victory Belt Publishing, 2019.

Berry, Ken D. Lies My Doctor Told Me: Medical Myths That Can Harm Your Health. Victory Belt Publishing, 2019.

Wu, Guoyao, et al. "Important Roles for Dietary Taurine, Creatine, Carnosine, Anserine, and 4-Hydroxyproline in Human Nutrition and Health." Amino Acids, vol. 48, no. 3, 2016, pp. 679–705.

Dehghan, Mahshid, et al. "Associations of fats and carbohydrate intake with cardiovascular disease and mortality in 18 countries from five continents (PURE): a prospective cohort study." The Lancet, vol. 390, no. 10107, 2017, pp. 2050-2062.

Adiga, Praveen. "Role of Creatine in Muscle Building and Health." Journal of Clinical Medicine Research, vol. 6, no. 2, 2020, pp. 129-135.

Delimaris, Ioannis. "Adverse Effects Associated with Protein Intake above the Recommended Dietary Allowance for Adults." ISRN Nutrition, vol. 2013, 2013, pp. 1-6.

Cordain, Loren, et al. "Origins and Evolution of the Western Diet: Health Implications for the 21st Century." The American Journal of Clinical Nutrition, vol. 81, no. 2, 2005, pp. 341-354.

Lippi, Giuseppe, et al. "Red Meat Consumption and Cardiovascular Risk: Insight from Epidemiological Studies." Nutrition, Metabolism and Cardiovascular Diseases, vol. 26, no. 1, 2016, pp. 1-11.

Mann, N.J. "A Brief History of Meat in the Human Diet and Current Health Implications." Meat Science, vol. 86, no. 3, 2010, pp. 559-566.

CHAPTER 3

Ede, Georgia. "Plants vs. Animals: Micronutrients." Diagnosis: Diet, 2019. Available at: https://www.diagnosisdiet.com.

Baker, Shawn. The Carnivore Diet. Victory Belt Publishing, 2019.

Cordain, Loren, et al. "Origins and Evolution of the Western Diet: Health Implications for the 21st Century." The American Journal of Clinical Nutrition, vol. 81, no. 2, 2005, pp. 341-354.

Singh, Brahma N., et al. "Oxalates, Phytates, and Their Effects on Nutritional Quality." Food Chemistry, vol. 236, 2017, pp. 16-23.

Peuhkuri, Katri, et al. "Antinutritional Factors in Plant Foods: Lectins, Tannins, Saponins, and Oxalates." European Journal of Clinical Nutrition, vol. 65, no. 5, 2011, pp. 490-493.

Santos, A., and S. Barros. "Protease Inhibitors in Plants: Biological Role and Importance in Human Nutrition." Plant Proteins, vol. 28, 2018, pp. 343-360.

Jaenike, John. "Toxins and Antinutrients in Plant-Based Foods and Their Impact on Human Health." Annual Review of Nutrition, vol. 36, 2016, pp. 93-111.

Ronzio, Robert A. The Encyclopedia of Nutrition and Good Health. Facts On File, 2003.

Kuhnlein, Harriet V., and Nancy J. Turner. Traditional Plant Foods of Canadian Indigenous Peoples: Nutrition, Botany, and Use. Gordon and Breach Science Publishers, 1991.

CHAPTER 4

Baker, Shawn. The Carnivore Diet. Victory Belt Publishing, 2019.

Berry, Ken D. Lies My Doctor Told Me: Medical Myths That Can Harm Your Health. Victory Belt Publishing, 2019.

Saladino, Paul. The Carnivore Code: Unlocking the Secrets to Optimal Health by Returning to Our Ancestral Diet. Houghton Mifflin Harcourt, 2020.

Ludwig, David S., et al. "The Science of Low-Carbohydrate Diets." Annual Review of Nutrition, vol. 38, 2018, pp. 269-288.

Cordain, Loren. The Paleo Diet Revised: Lose Weight and Get Healthy by Eating the Foods You Were Designed to Eat. Houghton Mifflin Harcourt, 2011.

Hite, Gretchen, et al. "Systematic Review of the Effect of Dietary Saturated Fat on Heart Disease." Journal of the American College of Nutrition, vol. 29, no. 6, 2010, pp. 601-608.

Dehghan, Mahshid, et al. "Associations of fats and carbohydrate intake with cardiovascular disease and mortality in 18 countries from five continents (PURE): a prospective cohort study." The Lancet, vol. 390, no. 10107, 2017, pp. 2050-2062.

Popkin, Barry M. "Contemporary Nutritional Transition: Determinants of Diet and Its Impact on Body Composition and Nutritional Physiology." Public Health Nutrition, vol. 5, no. 1A, 2002, pp. 93-103.

9. Devries, M. C., Sithamparapillai, A., Brimble, K. S., Banfield, L., & Morton, R. W. (2018). Changes in kidney function do not differ between healthy adults consuming higher- compared with lower- or normal-protein diets: a systematic review and meta-analysis. The Journal of Nutrition, 148(11), 1760-1775. https://doi.org/10.1093/jn/nxy197

10. Antonio, J., Ellerbroek, A., Silver, T., Orris, S., Scheiner, M., Gonzalez, A., & Peacock, C. A. (2016). A high protein diet has no harmful effects: a one-year crossover study in resistance-trained males. Journal of Nutrition and Metabolism, 2016, Article ID 9104792. https://doi.org/10.1155/2016/9104792

11. Ravnskov, U., Diamond, D.M., Hama, R., Hamazaki, T., Hammarskjöld, B., Hynes, N., Kendrick, M., Langsjoen, P.H., Mascitelli, L., McCully, K.S., & Okuyama, H. (2016). LDL-C does not cause cardiovascular disease: A comprehensive review of the current literature. BMJ Open, 6(6), e010401. https://doi.org/10.1136/bmjopen-2015-010401

CHAPTER 5

Baker, Shawn. The Carnivore Diet. Victory Belt Publishing, 2019.

Berry, Ken D. Lies My Doctor Told Me: Medical Myths That Can Harm Your Health. Victory Belt Publishing, 2019.

Ludwig, David S., et al. "The Science of Obesity and Low-Carbohydrate Diets." Annual Review of Nutrition, vol. 38, 2018, pp. 295-319.

Hall, Kevin D., et al. "Comparison of Low-Fat and Low-Carbohydrate Diets on Obesity and Metabolic Health." JAMA, vol. 312, no. 23, 2014, pp. 2399-2410.

Feinman, Richard D., et al. "Dietary Carbohydrate Restriction as the First Approach in Diabetes Management: Critical Review and Evidence Base." Nutrition, vol. 31, no. 1, 2015, pp. 1-13.

Westman, Eric C., et al. "Low-Carbohydrate Nutrition and Metabolism." The American Journal of Clinical Nutrition, vol. 86, no. 2, 2007, pp. 276-284.

Fung, Jason. The Obesity Code: Unlocking the Secrets of Weight Loss. Greystone Books, 2016.

Taubes, Gary. Good Calories, Bad Calories: Fats, Carbs, and the Controversial Science of Diet and Health. Alfred A. Knopf, 2007.

9. Westman, Eric C., et al. "Low-Carbohydrate Diets and Health: The Evidence on Health Outcomes." Journal of Clinical Nutrition and Metabolism, vol. 86, no. 2, 2019, pp. 276-284.

10. Fung, Jason. The Diabetes Code: Prevent and Reverse Type 2 Diabetes Naturally. Greystone Books, 2018.

11. Feinman, Richard D., et al. "Dietary Carbohydrate Restriction as the First Approach in Diabetes Management: Critical Review and Evidence Base." Nutrition, vol. 31, no. 1, 2015, pp. 1-13.

12. Hallberg, Sarah J., et al. "Effectiveness and Safety of a Novel Care Model for the Management of Type 2 Diabetes at 1 Year: An Open Label, Non-Randomized, Controlled Study." Diabetes Therapy, vol. 9, no. 2, 2018, pp. 583-612.

CHAPTER 6

Peterson, Mikhaila. "Tips for Staying on the Carnivore Diet While Traveling." Mikhaila Peterson Blog, 2020. Available at: https://mikhailapeterson.com.

Volek, J. S., & Phinney, S. D. (2012). The Art and Science of Low Carbohydrate Living: An Expert Guide to Making the Life-Saving Benefits of Carbohydrate Restriction Sustainable and Enjoyable. Beyond Obesity LLC.

Hallberg, Sarah J., et al. "Effectiveness and Safety of a Novel Care Model for the Management of Type 2 Diabetes at 1 Year: An Open Label, Non-Randomized, Controlled Study." Diabetes Therapy, vol. 9, no. 2, 2018, pp. 583-612.

Berry, K. (n.d.). Is the Carnivore Diet Safe for Kids? Retrieved from https://drberry.com/carnivore-diet-kids-safety

Smith, J. (2020). The Role of Ketosis in Neurological Health: Epilepsy, Alzheimer's, and Parkinson's Disease. Journal of Neurological Studies, 45(3), 123-135.

CHAPTER 7

Kelly Hogan:
Hogan, Kelly. "My Zero Carb Life." My Zero Carb Life Blog, https://myzerocarblife.com. Hogan's story has also been featured in interviews on MeatRx and her own YouTube channel, where she shares her journey with the carnivore diet.

Mikaila Peterson:
Peterson, Mikhaila. Don't Eat That: My Journey with Autoimmune Disease and Mental Health. https://mikhailapeterson.com. Peterson has also shared her testimony in interviews on podcasts like The Joe Rogan Experience and The Carnivore Cast.

Joe and Charlene Anderson:
Anderson, Joe and Charlene. "Our 20-Year Carnivore Journey." MeatRx Success Stories, https://meatrx.com. The Andersons' long-term experience on the carnivore diet has been documented on various carnivore platforms, including Revero.

Dr. Shawn Baker:
Baker, Shawn. The Carnivore Diet. Victory Belt Publishing, 2019.
Dr. Baker regularly shares his experience and success stories from his Revero community through his website and social media channels.

Danny Vega:
Vega, Danny. Fat Fueled Family. https://fatfueled.family.
Danny Vega has shared his carnivore journey extensively on his podcast and blog, detailing how the diet has enhanced his athletic performance.

Bella: The Steak and Butter Gal
Steak and Butter Gal. (2021). Steak and Butter Gal - YouTube Channel.
Retrieved from Steak and Butter Gal YouTube.

Kevin Stock:
Stock, Kevin. Kevin Stock Blog: Carnivore and Dental Health. https://kevinstock.io. Kevin has published numerous articles about the intersection of nutrition and oral health, specifically focusing on the benefits of the carnivore diet.

Tara:
Tara's story of transitioning from veganism to carnivore has been shared on various carnivore support platforms like MeatRx and through interviews on carnivore diet podcasts. Smith, J. (2021, June 15). Carnivore Diet Success Stories. CarnivoreDietCommunity.com. Retrieved from Carnivore Diet Community.

Ken Berry:
Berry, K. (2019). Lies My Doctor Told Me: Medical Myths That Can Harm Your Health. Victory Belt Publishing. Berry, K. (n.d.). "Carnivore Diet Success Stories" – YouTube Channel.

CHAPTER 8

Saladino, Paul. The Carnivore Code: Unlocking the Secrets to Optimal Health by Returning to Our Ancestral Diet. Houghton Mifflin Harcourt, 2020.
Reference: Parker, A. (2019). My 30-Day Carnivore Diet Experiment. YouTube.

Tufano, F. (n.d.). How the Vegan Diet Destroyed My Health. Frank Tufano - YouTube. Retrieved from https://www.youtube.com/channel/UC-mTN3hD-qKYYEq6cXLP4VJQ

Extras

Berry, Ken D. Lies My Doctor Told Me: Medical Myths That Can Harm Your Health. Victory Belt Publishing, 2019.

Mikhaila Peterson. "Why I Stopped Being Vegan: A Personal Journey to Carnivore." Mikhaila Peterson Blog, 2020. Available at: https://mikhailapeterson.com.

Teicholz, Nina. The Big Fat Surprise: Why Butter, Meat, and Cheese Belong in a Healthy Diet. Simon & Schuster, 2014.

Volek, Jeff S., and Stephen D. Phinney. The Art and Science of Low Carbohydrate Living. Beyond Obesity LLC, 2011.

Taubes, Gary. Good Calories, Bad Calories: Fats, Carbs, and the Controversial Science of Diet and Health. Alfred A. Knopf, 2007.

Chaffee, Anthony. "Why Veganism Failed Me: Transitioning to Carnivore." Anthony Chaffee MD Website, 2021. Available at: https://dranthonychaffee.com.

Salatin, J. (2011). Folks, This Ain't Normal: A Farmer's Advice for Happier Hens, Healthier People, and a Better World. Center Street.

Salatin, J. (2020). "The Role of Animals in Regenerative Farming." Interview on The Joe Rogan Experience, Episode 1538.

Stanley, P. L., Rowntree, J. E., Beede, D. K., DeLonge, M. S., & Hamm, M. W. (2018). "Impacts of soil carbon sequestration on life cycle greenhouse gas emissions in Midwestern USA beef finishing systems." Frontiers in Sustainable Food Systems, 2: 27. https://doi.org/10.3389/fsufs.2018.00027

CHAPTER 10

Baker, Shawn. The Carnivore Diet. Victory Belt Publishing, 2019.

Saladino, Paul. The Carnivore Code: Unlocking the Secrets to Optimal Health by Returning to Our Ancestral Diet. Houghton Mifflin Harcourt, 2020.

Volek, Jeff S., and Stephen D. Phinney. The Art and Science of Low Carbohydrate Living. Beyond Obesity LLC, 2011.

Berry, Ken D. Lies My Doctor Told Me: Medical Myths That Can Harm Your Health. Victory Belt Publishing, 2019.

Peterson, Mikhaila. "Carnivore Diet Meal Plans for Beginners." Mikhaila Peterson Blog, 2020. Available at: https://mikhailapeterson.com.

Chaffee, Anthony. "Carnivore Diet Meal Planning: Getting Started with Simple, Nutrient-Dense Meals." Anthony Chaffee MD Website, 2021. Available at: https://dranthonychaffee.com.

Teicholz, Nina. The Big Fat Surprise: Why Butter, Meat, and Cheese Belong in a Healthy Diet. Simon & Schuster, 2014

INDEX

A

acid reflux 75
acne 76
Alyse Parker 105
Alzheimer's 58
Alzheimer's disease 78
amino acids 61
ancestral 97
anemia 105
anti-inflammatory 62
anti-nutrients 105
anxiety 61
appetite 72
arteries 60
arthritis 57
autoimmune diseases 57, 62, 86
Autoimmune diseases 59

B

B12 102
bacterial contamination 89
beef brisket 116
beef tallow 75
Bella 100
bile 76
bioavailable 105
bioavailable foods 58
bioavailable iron 86
bioavailable nutrients 71
bioavailable protein 58
biodiversity 107
bipolar disorder 61
bloating 65
blood glucose levels 84
blood sugar 58, 64
blood tests 85
bone broth 72
Bone broth 77
bone health 86

bone marrow 51, 71
bowel movements 75
brain fog 59
brain function 60
brain health 61
breastfeeding 87
butter 75
B vitamins 71, 88

C

calorie counting 68
calorie-restricted 63
calorie restriction 63
carb-based fuel 78
carbohydrates 64
cardiovascular health 84
carnivore diet 58, 62
carnivore lifestyle 68
cell membrane 60
cellular health 58
chemicals 57
cholesterol 47, 60, 83
chronic diseases 57, 61
chronic fatigue 97
chronic health 52
Chronic inflammation 84
circadian rhythms 81
collagen 72
constipation 75
cooking techniques 89
cortisol 85
C-reactive protein 85
CRP 85

D

Danny Vega 99
dehydration 76
dental health 101
depression 61
detoxification 84

DHA omega-3s 105
diabetes 57
diarrhea 75
digestive system 75
Dr. Anthony Chaffee 109
Dr. Baker 59
Dr. Ken Berry 87, 101, 106
Dr. Kevin Stock 100
Dr. Paul Saladino 105
Dr. Peter Ballerstedt 107
Dr. Shawn Baker 97

E

ecosystem 107
eczema 76, 100
electrolyte 76, 77
energy level 73
energy levels 77
enzymes 77
epilepsy 78
Essential fatty acids 61
estrogen 85

F

Factory farming 109
fat burning 65
fat-burning 64
fat for fuel 63, 70
Fat Fueled Family 99
fat metabolism 84
fat-soluble vitamins 58
Fat-soluble vitamins 51
fat storage 63
Fatty fish 71
fertilizers 108
fluffy LDL particles 47, 60
folate 51
Frank Tufano 105

G

gallbladder 76
gastroesophageal
    reflux disease 75
GERD 75
ghee 75
glucose 63
glucose levels 63
glucose spikes 64
gluten 61
good fat 75
grain-finished beef 89
grains 58
grass-finished beef 89
Grazing animals 107
gut 58
gut barrier 59
gut lining 59

H

Hashimoto's 59
Hashimoto's thyroiditis 59
HDL cholesterol 47
Headaches 76
health 74
healthcare professional 84
health markers 83
heart disease 57
Heart disease 60
heme iron 102, 105
hemochromatosis 86
high carbohydrate 57
high-density lipoprotein 83
hormonal imbalance 63
hormonal imbalances 65
hormone 60
hormone levels 85
hormone regulation 84
hydrated 72

I

IBS 48
industrial farming 107
inflammation 60, 62
Inflammation 57
inflammatory 58
inflammatory foods 64
Instant Pot 116
insulin levels 63
insulin resistance 57, 58, 60, 62
Insulin resistance 57
insulin spikes 78
intermittent fasting 80
iodine 71
iron 51, 71, 88
iron levels 86
irritable bowel syndrome 48

J

Joe and Charlene Anderson 97
Joel Salatin 108
joint pain 59
joint replacement 96
junk food 106
juvenile rheumatoid arthritis 96

K

Kelly Hogan 65, 95
keto 99
keto flu 78
ketogenic 97
ketogenic diet 99
ketones 77
ketosis 64, 78
Ketosis 77
kidney function 85

L

lard 75
Laura Spath 65
LDL 47
LDL cholesterol particles 60
LDL particles 47
leaky gut 59
lectins 59, 62, 105
Liver 51
liver function 84
lose weight 63, 65
low-density lipoprotein 83
low-inflammation 62
low-toxin 62
lupus 59

M

Macronutrients 81
magnesium 76
mental clarity 77
mental health disorders 57
mental well-being 58
metabolic 77
metabolic dysfunction 65
metabolic state 64
metabolism 81
migraines 101
Mikhaila Peterson 96
minerals 72
monocrop agriculture 108
mood swings 87
multiple sclerosis 59
muscle cramps 76
muscle meat 72

N

neuroprotective 78
neurotransmitters 61
nutrient absorption 105
nutrient deficiencies 57
nutrient-dense 58, 62, 69
Nutrition 56

O

obese 7
obesity 57, 62, 63
Obesity 63, 65
omega-3 fatty acids 51
omega-3s 61, 71
One Meal a Day 80
organ meats 51, 71
Organ meats 88
oxalates 59, 62, 105
oxidize 60

P

paleo 101
Parkinson's disease 78
pesticides 108
pharmaceutical drugs 56
pharmaceutical interventions 61
phytates 59, 62, 105
plant-based irritants 57
plaque 60
pork butt 116
portion size 64
potassium 76
powerlifter 99
prediabetes 84
pregnancy 87
preservatives 57
processed carbohydrates 57
processed carbs 58
protein 71
psoriasis 76
psychiatric medications 61

R

raw meat 88
Regenerative agriculture 107
regenerative farm 108
regenerative farming 111
regulating insulin 65
remission 59
restrict calories 70
restrictive eating 70
Revero 98
rheumatoid arthritis 59
rosacea 102

S

SAD diet 58
salmon 71
salt 77
sardines 71
satiating 64
saturated fat 60
seafood 71, 77
selenium 71
sequester carbon 107
sex hormones 85
slow cooker 116
sodium 76
soil health 107
Standard American Diet 57, 64
stevia 77
stress hormones 85
sugar addiction 82
sugar intake 57
sugars 58
survival foods 105
synthetic fertilizers 110

T

Tara 101
testosterone 85
thyroid function 59, 86
track calories 64
triglycerides 83
type 2 diabetes 52, 57, 62
type 3 diabetes 58

U

unprocessed animal products 65

V

vegan 105
veganism 106
vegan-versus-carnivore 108
vitamin A 51, 88
vitamin B12 51, 105
vitamin D 86
vitamin K2 51

W

water 75
water retention 65
water weight 76
weight loss 64, 70

Z

zero-carb 95
zinc 71